The Church

The Church

Are Christian's Winning Or Losing The Battle?

Samuel D. Scull

WestBow
PRESS
A DIVISION OF THOMAS NELSON

WestBow Press books may be ordered through booksellers or by contacting:

*WestBow Press
A Division of Thomas Nelson
1663 Liberty Drive
Bloomington, IN 47403
www.westbowpress.com
1-(866) 928-1240*

ISBN: 978-1-4497-4515-8 (sc)

Library of Congress Control Number: 2012905687

Printed in the United States of America

WestBow Press rev. date: 4/20/2013

TABLE OF CONTENTS

AUTHOR'S PREFACE

Praise the Lord and pass the ammunition and get ready for war because time is running out. Prophecy is being fulfilled right before our eyes and some Christians don't know or are afraid to accept the truth of God's word. Many Christians and secular people are going to be surprised when things begin to happen. The question is who is correct about where the church is, and will be before, during and after the tribulation period? I understand there are three thoughts about the Tribulation period and the church. Some say the church will be called out before the tribulation (called pre-tribulation.). Others say the church will go through half of the seven years of tribulation (called mid. tribulation.). And still others say the church will go through all seven years of the tribulation (called post tribulation.). Who is right? There have been many Christian authors write about all three. There are others who will say none of these are right and give their rendition of how it will happen. I suggest you start studying and putting things into context, God will show you. I thought I might share some thoughts about the subject, but, maybe in another book. In this book I will be writing about other subjects that have concerned me over the years. Most of what you will read in this book comes from seventy years of exposure to the Pentecostal way of believing.

During the nineties God started dealing with me through His Holy Spirit about certain scriptures that I've had a difficult time with over the years. I read scriptures and a few books on one subject I want to talk about. These particular scripture interpretations were taught to me by Pentecostal ministers and teachers. I attended only Pentecostal churches from my childhood and was indoctrinated into believing what was being taught and how these scriptures were being interpreted by most Pentecostals. I was always taught that the Pentecostal way of believing was the true way. I shared this belief with many people for years believing it was the truth. As the years passed it bothered my spirit because of what I observed happening in the church didn't always match the scriptures. How could all other denominations be wrong in their interpretations and the Pentecostals be right? The content of this book is not just about the Pentecostal church, but, the whole church (body of Christ) and why there is no unity.

Remember, my sentiment over the years of God's church (meaning all Christian churches) is somewhat negative when it comes to their interpretation of God's word. My concern has always been if their interpretations are different and they are reading the same Bible, who is telling the truth? Sounds like confusion to me. I believe most church doctrine comes from mans interpretation with no help from the Holy Spirit. I will explain how I feel that some politicians and intellectuals have corrupted the church (body of Christ). Man has made it so easy in his interpretation that we people of many different personalities can decide which one fits our lifestyle and believe we are okay with God.

This Country was founded by people with deep convictions about their freedoms, one being the freedom of religion. The history of the church in this country is very interesting and I recommend all Christians read about it. I started asking God what was needed to help Christians move towards unity in such a diverse system. The reason for asking God about this is because I don't see any movement of unity between most Christian churches. I understand there are Ministerial Groups in the Christian communities, but nothing is done about developing unity within the church (body of Christ). Ministers or laymen will get together from different churches for fellowship, but will not discuss their doctrine and why they are so different. Unity is the state of being one or united, and the quality of being one in spirit; harmony and agreement. Everyone should drop their intellectual prowess and start being serious about reaching unity within the church (body of Christ). I know there are some Bible Scholars that say this unity between the different Christian churches will never happen. Is what God's word says about church unity mean as long as we all believe in salvation we are in unity, or does it mean all Christians will be in unity when they all agree together and live under one truth, given by the Holy Spirit, not man?

My concerns are focusing on things I believe are wrong within our Christian church and not pointing the finger at anyone in particular. What I'm about to share will seem strange to many, but I believe this is what God is showing me. God has a supernatural way of doing things that some Christians don't understand. After much exposure and being concerned about some church doctrines over the years I felt obligated to share my understanding of some of the scriptures and their interpretation. So this is what I am doing and God continues to show me the truth. I have shared this truth with Bible study groups, some ministers, and whoever wanted to listen. I know it's difficult to accept a different view about a doctrine that has been taught you for many years and you thoroughly believed in it. All I ask is for everyone to read what God is showing me, study it, and let God's word (not man) be your guide.

My aim here is to have you read God's word and analyze what I'm saying. Don't let me lead you down a path you think is wrong. You search the scriptures with an open mind on things I say and believe, and ask God to show you whether it is the truth or not. One of the things I have observed over the years about people is, they go to church and agree or disagree with what is being taught, but, some never study God's word to test the messenger (minister). Some believe whatever the minister says is gospel. They are right when they say a minister called by God should know and tell the truth, but we Christians should always test the minister to make sure. There are too many false ministers in our churches today.

I pray that people will study, test the teacher, and help get the church on the right path to building unity in the Body of Christ. I just recently heard a Baptist Minister put down Pentecostals because they speak in tongues, calling them all kinds of nasty names. This is not the way to treat other Christians that you believe are wrong. We are supposed to be winning souls for Christ not condemning our brothers and sisters in Christ who you believe are misinterpreting

God's word. The right way to address the differences is we all need to study God's word on the subject, let the Holy Spirit guide you to the truth. Then we need to have a meeting with them, an open discussion about what God has shown you about the subject. Do it God's way, through love, not arrogance. And also do it with an open heart and mind using the Holy Spirit as your guide. You might be right, and then again, you might be wrong.

As I've said, I am not pointing the finger at anyone in particular. I'm doing the same as many ministers do. I'm talking to God, studying His word and trying to share things that I believe has gone wrong with the church over the years and still does in some cases. So, if something strikes you wrong, like I'm pointing my finger, please pray and take another look at what I'm saying. I'm not trying to be dogmatic, I just want to help the church understand what God is showing me are some mistakes being made and how some scriptures are being taught wrong.

Some might say this book is nothing but my ideas of how the church should be operated and they have a right to say that, but don't just read the book, compare what I say with God's word first before judging me. The stories are true. Whether we like it or not we are in this boat together, and without each other we will all sink. I have always lived my life with this thought in mind. When involved in any task, whether it's in the Armed Forces, playing sports, working in an educational system, factory, chemical plant, auto plant or anything having to do with people, even church, if we can't work as a team, it doesn't work. Teamwork builds unity.

INTRODUCTION

This book is being written because I have had concerns over the years about how the church has drifted away from its original assignment given by God. Some of the chapters are true stories and others are only my opinion. I prayed, studied and God has given me some answers to why this has happened. I finally resolved to the fact that God talks to all born again Christians, not just a few as some would like you to believe. We all have the same opportunity to come before Him with our questions and concerns. This book is not a long read, but, a book that God impressed on me to write and share with others. Some of the chapters are only about how things have happened over the years that have done damage to the church (body of Christ). These things might not happen in all churches but I would venture to say it does in most of them. After all we are all human, we make mistakes and believe we can do things better than everyone else. The things that I talk about have destroyed and divided many churches. When listening to what is being taught or just discussing His word with Biblical scholars, some of the answers I receive never seem to match what I read and understand about God's word. God says to study and show yourself approved, meaning, don't just listen to the teacher or preacher, but read and study the word yourself and discuss it with others who are doing the same. After doing all of that, pray and ask God's Holy Spirit to guide you in the truth.

Another reason for writing this book is because I want to know and share the truth. God is showing me through His Holy Spirit that the church is failing to tell the whole truth. Have you ever stopped to think of all the different denominations and variations of teaching there are in the United States and why there are so many different interpretations of Gods written word? This is not what God wants. Apparently this is what man wants. Out of all these different denominations, which one is telling the truth? I know this is what Satan wants and this will continue until man recognizes his deceitful methods. Each denomination will say they are right and the others are wrong. The problem with this is, some Christians don't read, study, or discuss His word to find the truth. So wipe the dust off your Bible and take this trip with me through His word. I believe there are many misinterpretations of some of the scriptures. Because most people only take the word of man without reading the word of God for themselves has allowed the church (body of Christ) to become so splintered.

The stories I share in this book concerning things happening in Christian churches and how the church has been operating in the past and continues today comes from comparing them to God's word. This book reflects my sentiments on the Christian church in general. Some of my remarks will resonate with you and other remarks won't. It is okay to disagree, because some people reading this might attend a different denomination or may not have these same situations occur. As I said earlier I believe the things I talk about happens in most churches. That is why I want to share with you what I believe is only mans interpretations of God's word on certain scriptures. All I ask of you is to pray and put some spiritual thought into what I'm saying, asking for God's guidance.

There are a few things I want to make sure you understand before you read this book. I am not a Doctor of Divinity, but, I do have an Associate Degree in Bible Theology. I have been exposed to the Bible for about seventy years. This is not something new to me, but, I still struggle with some scriptures and continue to ask God for the answers. I am not bragging because of my church background or my knowledge of some scriptures. There are many different interpretations of God's word and I understand some, but not all. I only want to express my concern and give my opinion about how I believe man has messed things up in some churches. I grew up in the Pentecostal church and learned about Jesus Christ and what He did for us as a human race. The Pentecostal denomination is young compared to other mainline denominations. I believe the movement started back in the late 19th and early 20th centuries. Some might say it started on the day of Pentecost and not to many years later the Roman Catholic Church put a stop to many of the doctrines. I will try to explain this later in one of the chapters. Attending a church that people from other denominations made fun of because of their doctrine has always concerned me. I understand how Pentecostals are viewed by other denominations and in some respect, I understand why. I believe my exposure to the Pentecostal church doctrine and with the help of the Holy Spirit is enough for me to share an understanding on whether their interpretation on certain scriptures is correct when comparing it to God's word.

CHAPTER ONE

MY BELIEFS IN WHAT GOD'S WORD SAYS

I believe it is important when you are a writer, teacher, pastor, or someone just sharing, or discussing God's word with others, to let everyone know what your beliefs are. I have observed some Christians over the years that are very reluctant and private about expressing their true beliefs about God's word. Some Christians, including ministers, will express their denominational beliefs, but not their personal beliefs. Some will pick and choose what they want to believe without any discussion with other Christians to make sure they are on God's path of truth. I only believe what comes from the Bible (King James) and not from any other books that claim they are true. When people can take God's Word and claim God was wrong in the way it was written and add their thoughts and beliefs on how it should have been are treading on thin ice. During the years of Muhammad (600AD) he didn't like the way it was written so he taught a different story and his followers wrote the Koran and replaced God with Allah. There is

1

no scripture in the Bible that calls God, Allah. Over the years man has taken the Bible, added to or taken away from God's truth. Some ministers don't believe or can even prove what they preach. When reading what I have written people will understand my beliefs having to do with God and His word.

It always amazes me when I listen to some pastors, evangelist, and teachers, because what they say doesn't really match God's word. Understanding God's word as a layperson concerning leadership and only God can call you, you would expect them to be right on target. If you interrupt them to show them their mistake (which is biblical), they become shocked, mad and embarrassed, and people look at you like your crazy. If you don't address the situation immediately the truth might never come out, and if you're right they will continue to tell a lie. I know there are people that will disagree with everything I say about my beliefs but I don't see any other belief system that will give you eternal life with the creator. No matter how much man has done to denigrate Christianity and man has done their best, it still has the best outcome of all religions and that is what we all should want.

1. I believe in God and His Trinity, God the Father, God the Son, and God the Holy Spirit. God, the Father of creation is setting on His Throne in Heaven with his Son Jesus at His right hand. His Holy Spirit is with Christians here on earth today as our comforter and guide.

2. I believe in creation, and God creating man in His own image. I believe the creation of the universe by God took

place many years before the creation of man as Christians have been taught from Geneses 1. I believe Lucifer was the first Adam that ruled the world many-many years prior to the second Adam and his wife Eve. Adam and Eve allowed the first Adam (satan) to deceive them which allowed him to stay and compete for mans soul.

3. I believe Jesus Christ is God's Son. God the Father sent Him to earth as a human to save mankind from their sins. The sins of man were brought about by Lucifer (satan), the leader of the cons, who pulled the wool over Eve's eyes, and in turn duped Adam causing the trickle down effect on all man kind. This means "we all have sinned and come short of the glory of God", (Ro. 6:23 KJV). Because Jesus defeated satan and was crucified, took the stripes on His back, and hung on the cross shedding His blood for our sins, we can have eternal life with Him by just accepting Him as our savior. Jesus Christ could not be deceived by satan.

4. I believe everything the Bible says that God did in the Old and New Testaments. God gave us a beginning for eternal life with Him and we failed His only command, (not to eat the fruit of one tree), and because of mans sin He gave us an ending. After our failure He still gives us a way out to spend eternity with Him. That way is through Jesus Christ. He chose certain individuals (with His Spirit upon them) in the Old Testament to carry out His commands and teach the people about His word. He chose all Christians (born again in His Spirit) in the New Testament to carry out His commands and teach the people about His word. I don't believe we should pick and choose what to teach people

from His word. Doing this would create misunderstandings about God's intent for all of humanity.

5. I believe the Holy Spirit is God's power and this power was given to some people (not all) in the Old Testament, but is given to all people in the New Testament through the born again experience by accepting His Son as their savior. We can't have His spirit within us and not have His power. If God's power is not working in our lives we need to look in the mirror and ask what is wrong. God doesn't lie.

6. I believe God has made available to us the spiritual gifts of wisdom, knowledge, miracles, healings, tongues (languages), interpretation (of different languages and dreams), discernment of spirits, and prophecy. Does everyone get all? No! The Holy Spirit decides and guides, not man. These gifts were always available to people with the spirit upon them in the Old Testament and became available to all Christians at the day of Pentecost in the New Testament.

7. I believe in the baptism in the Holy Spirit and it occurs at regeneration. I believe when you repent of your sins and accept Jesus Christ as your savior you become a temple for His Holy Spirit. This means you have been baptized by God's spirit and been cleansed and purified, not by water, but, by the Holy Spirit and fire. John the Baptist said, I baptize you unto repentance, (using water as the cleansing and purifier as did all Old Testament baptisms). Water was used for cleansing everything including furniture in the Old Testament. John the Baptist said, but the one who follows will baptize you in the Holy Spirit and with fire

(using the Holy Spirit and fire as the cleansing and purifier, not water). I don't believe you need to seek a gift that has already been given. I will explain this in detail later in this book. Some denominations still believe that water baptism is still necessary, but I don't believe they can prove it from God's word. Jesus is the baptizer and He gave us the Holy Spirit to clean the vessel so He could use it as His temple.

8. I believe that all of God's word is for our use today, not just some of it. If we say some of it was for back when Christ was here, why was it put in the Bible for our use? I'll explain later why I believe leaders in the church have over the years been afraid to tell the truth about certain scriptures.

9. I believe Christians need to get serious and stop agreeing with everything that is being said by the church leaders (Pastors, Evangelist, Teachers, and Prophets). According to God's word they are appointed (called) by God. Read Ephesians. All that are chosen are to teach and perfect the saints, for the work of the ministry and for the edifying of the body of Christ. Christianity is not a game for all of the different denominations to compete for who becomes the largest and richest church. God does not care about our ego. He only cares about our souls. Christians have allowed the intellectuals and politicians to take control of the church. After all they believe they are more educated and know what is best for everyone, because they understand God's word and you don't. All I ever heard in the churches I attended was bragging about how the denomination was growing and building new churches. Their was very little talk about how many souls have been won for Christ or how many saints have been educated for the ministry and sent out. There is

too much emphases put on congregation size and wealth and not enough put on salvation. Some ministers (pastors) are more interested in asking and looking for more money then souls. That is absolutely wrong! Winning souls is more important to God then all the money in the world. If more money is needed to live on (not wasted on earthy things) you better ask God. He will supply all our needs.

10. I believe we need to be educated, but having a Collage Degree has nothing to do with understanding God's word. Praying and asking God to open our eyes and mind to understanding is what we need to do to gain wisdom and knowledge of His word. God's word says to study to show thyself approved, not to study to become intellectuals. If all Christians would just study His word, the people in the leadership would learn to respect others. Leaders would then take notice and you would see a difference in church attendance. We would see things happening according to God's word because we got serious and God would be pleased. Educating Christians to be intellectuals is the wrong way to go. Educating Christians to understand God's word and how to lead sinners to Christ is the right way to go. Just remember, walking the walk is just as important as talking the talk. The world knows a hypocrite when they see one.

CHAPTER TWO

GOD'S CALL ON YOUR LIFE

WHO CALLS MEN INTO THE MINISTRY, GOD OR MAN?

In the late nineties God impressed on me to return to a specific church after a long absence and shortly after returning, it was evident why. When reading the scriptures, I felt as though I was living back in the time of the Corinthian Church. God started showing me that some of the sermons, communion, worship, and gifts of the Spirit being used were out of order according to scripture. These same things are still not right even though God is showing me how to deal with them. At first, I prayed and thought I could deal with the leadership in a way that was not offensive. I soon found out this was not working, so God told me to start using tough love. Some things did change, but not others. God says to me, be patient, and He will continue to deal with me in ways to continue what He has asked of me.

Sometimes we Christians get in a rut and blindness sets in. God is showing me the church in general is in that position. People who are aware of this are either living in fear or do not have the courage to address a bad situation. I am sharing this story with you as a Christian should. Too many times we Christians do not share enough of what God is doing in our lives so the whole body of Christ knows and understands. After all, isn't our main concern the proper function of the body of Christ? If we Christians go off on tangents and expect others in the Lord to agree and defend us without complete understanding, is very unfair. I've said in some communications to the church if only one side of the story is told, it's lacking balance, and you end up with Christians that are unbalanced in their understanding.

The question laymen need to ask a Minister is, were you called by God or did you just aspire to the position through church politics? A true Minister needs to ask the same question to any associate pastor. What I am about to share is not to agree or disagree or even deter someone from what God is asking them to do. I just want to point out how mans intellect can sometime get in the way of God moving in their life. I know some will want to challenge me and I will accept that if God's word is used to settle the challenge.

If an associate pastor says God is dealing with him about moving in another direction other than the vision at the local church he attends and he knows this would not be accepted by others, the road ahead would be rough. In his preparations for this move, my questions would be, did the person prepare the church in detail of what God was asking? Did the person ask the Senior Pastor for time to make a presentation before the elders, so they who represent the church would understand what God was asking him to do? Did he have a problem with the leadership and the direction they were leading the church? Was he under external pressure from family, relatives, or friends to start his own church with a slightly different doctrine? Is this an intellectual move (the leadership don't understand God's word like he dose)? Did he thoroughly discuss his interpretation of certain scriptures with the leadership or was he afraid to? Did he thoroughly explain to his immediate family what might happen if he takes this path? Was this moving towards a cult that he was getting involved in? A very important question, did he ask God for a conformation from another Christian that this is what God wanted him to do? Many more questions could be asked about why, but, lets see where this takes us.

I understand people who have held jobs over a period of time and become very good at what they do. An example would be if you worked in a law firm as a legal assistant without a degree you could end up thinking you know as much as the lawyer does. One problem with that is you think you know everything about the law and with some, the big ego shows up. You start trying to impress others about how much you know. This builds your ego to a point when reading the Bible you become very legalistic in your interpretations. God did not give us His word for lawyers to interpret for us. He made it so everyone would understand what He was saying by just asking the Holy Spirit to open their eyes and minds to understanding. We should never let our intellect think we know more then everyone else. You put yourself in the position of wanting everyone to start defining words like "IS". Remember that one. God is not a respecter of persons and He talks to all Christians, not just the intellectuals or politicians.

I remember when God talked to me when the church I was attending wanted to buy some property and could not afford the price the owners wanted at that time. God showed me how the church could purchase the property at the price they could afford and that was half of the original price. I shared this with the leaders of the church and the pastor shared this with their lawyer. I was told when presenting this to the lawyer he said he never heard of this approach before, for buying property, but when checking he found it legal. The church purchased the property and the owners were satisfied with how it was done. God works in strange ways and uses people that others sometime question, why?

I believe deep down in my heart when God wants you to do something, He will tell you through His Holy Spirit by vision or other means just exactly what to do and how to do it. He will not ask and then allow you to hang out on a limb. I am sharing this to show how God sometimes uses certain people through vision or study to help correct a particular situation. As Christians, we sometimes allow our personalities to get involved, instead of the Holy Spirit. God is showing me this has been and continues to be one of the main problems in the church. I am not questioning peoples calling (if truly by God), but, some people call themselves (their personality) into a situation and try to correct it. It won't work unless God calls you to help. God is beginning to use me through the gift of discerning and distinguishing between true and false spirits.

When reading about the differences this minister had with the main denominations it stirred some interest within me to take a further look into his material and compare it with what the scriptures say. After studying God's word, my first reaction was that he should take another look at what he was saying, but I decided to study more and educate myself and ask God to help me understand the truth. My first thought was, he wanted his own church where he could be in control. If he was in control he could fight the government about things he disagreed with having to do with church and state. There were laws he didn't like and he didn't want to follow them, and if followed he would be violating God's laws. This country was founded on the freedom of religion and allows all people to worship as they please. The United States of America is similar to the Roman Empire which also allowed missionaries to go out and share the word of God.

After meeting with this minister on two occasions I learned he wanted a tax free status for his church but didn't want to sign a document from the Government giving him that freedom. He wanted the tax free status but didn't want the Government to be in control. I agree the Government is trying to take to much control over our lives and our leaders in Congress need to put a stop to that. But the other side of this is, there are some scoundrels in our churches that need someone too oversee what they are doing. If the church can't do this, our Government should. We still live in a world controlled by secular people and some Christians, as they did in the 1st Century and this still continues today. What is important here is our country was founded by people who wanted to be free and not dictated to. They wanted the freedom to worship as they please and this is still one of the most important liberties we have. This country is a launching pad for sharing the gospel around the world and the secular government still allows the church to file for a tax-free status, even if they do have to sign a paper to receive a license. I believe this is important so we Christians can continue sharing Christ around the world without being suppressed by some dictator. This minister uses the one scripture that talks about bowing to two masters. Signing a piece of paper to allow the church to be tax-free is not bowing to another god, it is following the law established by our government. I know this minister follows other laws the government says we must follow. As Christians, we should thank God we still have these freedoms. Soon, it will come to an end.

If you don't like what the Government is doing and you want to take a stand on this by not signing a piece of paper to be tax exempt and you believe it will cause you to serve another master, you must take a stand against all civil authority. Put your case together and go to court. Just remember the law in this country is still the law and according to God's word we are to obey the law. This is a country of laws, and if you think Christians serve two masters by following its' laws, you're wrong. I do not serve two masters, I do not bow down to a President or anyone else in the federal or civil government, I only bow to my Lord and Savior, Jesus Christ. When Jesus returns, I will continue to obey His laws because they will be the only law here on earth. There will be no Government controlled by man. Jesus will be here and He is and will be our leader forever. In the meantime, Jesus wants us to obey the laws here on earth. Jesus followed the laws as did Peter, Paul, and many others. If you are determined to take this stand of what I believe is a misinterpretation of God's word, and you are saying Jesus was serving two masters because He instructed Peter to pay taxes that was owed Caesar according to the law, you will lose in court. Pay Caesar what is owed him.

I want to share the following because I feel this will help everyone understand why I believe it is important to put God's word in to context before going off on a tangent and dragging others with you. This is found in Matthew (KJV). In the New Testament a temple tax was a levy on Jewish males for the support of the temple. Jesus reminds Peter that Kings do not collect taxes from their own sons, but from the citizens not belonging to the royal family. Remember Peter and Jesus and all Christians are of the royal family of the Heavenly King, whose earthly habitation is the Temple. They are exempt from the temple tax. While not obligated to pay the tax, Jesus freely does to avoid giving offense. He who pays his tax is still the master of all things.

Peter was not satisfied and says "We must obey God rather than men" (KJV). But putting things into context this reaction must be balanced with what Peter also believed and later wrote, "Submit your-selves for the Lord's sake to every authority instituted among men" (KJV). I believe most world governments exist to restrain evil and some still don't. They try to commend those who do right. Most people are aware of the corruption in all fazes of government as Peter was aware of corruption in high places. As we submit to the laws of government and try our best to abstain from fleshly desires it will still pass away under the judgment of God.

Believers must never reject governmental authority. Unless I completely misunderstand God's word I do believe He wants us to obey the law. If He wants us to do this why would we be serving two masters? Everything we do as good citizens we do because of mans laws here on earth, so if we say by signing a document will cause us to serve two masters we better start disobeying all of mans laws now. If we don't we will be serving two masters in everything we do. If we can choose and pick which laws to follow or not to follow, we become hypocrites. As a Christian you not only misrepresent God but become that stumbling block to many others taking them down the wrong path. As far as I can see by signing this document we are not denying God as our master, but only following mans law, which is a requirement until Christ returns. This does not make man our master.

CHAPTER THREE

STUDY TO SHOW THYSELF APPROVED

I believe Jesus Christ studied to show himself approved (by His Father) while here on earth, but He never looked down on people and He surely wouldn't call anyone stupid. He also picked a team to carry on His work, and they were not all intellectuals. Jesus took his education and became a servant of the people. One of the most important things the church has forgotten is that Jesus Christ is in charge and chooses who he wants in leadership rolls, not always the intellectual man. Maybe the leaders in the church (body of Christ) should start over by re-reading His Word and structure the church properly.

I do believe in education, but I also believe if people without an expensive education can read and study God's word with an honest heart and open mind, He will allow them to see the truth. It is not the intellectual part of the person that God is interested in, it's their heart and soul. I believe we are coming to a point in time in our society when people with the higher education that consider themselves intellectuals will start calling people without the same education, stupid. I've already seen signs of this coming from some intellectuals that appear fairly regular on TV news shows. A High School education might not elevate you to an intellectual status unless you were born with exceptional learning skills. These highly educated people will eventually wake up and agree that these people they called stupid still continue to protect them, save their lives and keep them free. This will be done by some educated people and lesser educated people paying more attention to what God's word says and less about what the intellectual man says. I could share many stories about some intellectual types I worked with and went to church with that would scare the life out of you because of their way of thinking.

I wonder how many Christians believe they should study to show thy-self approved? I wonder how many Christians accept the words of their leaders as the truth, without studying, to verify whether it is the truth or not? Are Christians going to say to God when standing before Him on Judgment day, I just took their word as Gospel without studying it for myself to verify the truth? His word says to study to show thyself (not someone else) approved. It says in Matt. 7:15; (KJV) "Beware of false prophets". One way to expose them is to compare what they say to God's word allowing the Holy Spirit to guide you in the truth.

God's word has many scriptures relating to knowledge and wisdom, and if you desire them, they will only come by reading His word. These are gifts that God will give us through the guidance of His Holy Spirit, but He also says to study to show thy-self approved. In Romans 15:4 (KJV) it says, "For whatsoever things were written aforetime were written for our learning, that we through patience and comfort of the Scriptures might have hope". God wants us to be wise by seeking guidance in everything we say and do through His word. In Ps. 27:11(KJV) it says "Teach me thy way, O Lord and lead me in the plain path". God wants us to travel down the right path. In Proverbs 2:5-6 (KJV), it says, "Then shalt thou understand the fear of the Lord, and find the knowledge of God. For the Lord giveth wisdom: out of His mouth cometh knowledge and understanding".

The truth on any subject that God has written will only be understood by comparing all scriptures relating to the same subject. God will do what you ask by allowing His Holy Spirit to help you understand all scriptures. All subjects need to be proven by His Word before you teach or preach them. This means you should pray and ask God to show you what Ministers and Elders you should discuss His word with. By doing it this way you will make sure it's coming from God and not you. Mans ego has a tendency to want praise for everything he does, instead of giving all the praise to God. I believe this is one reason why the church is in trouble. So many ministers use their own interpretations without sharing it with the elders or other true men of God (not the church politicians) for conformation. I suggest all ministers take another look at the path they have taken or are about to take and then pray and re-read God's word to help them stay true. Many others will follow them down that path so it is important that it's the right one. They will eventually answer to God for everyone they guided down that path, whether right or wrong.

In order to rightly divide the word of truth on any subject, people need to take all the scriptures on a given subject and study them in the light of all the Bible has to say on that subject. If you have a revelation from God about the word, prove it scripturally. Then you should submit it to others of established reputation in the body of Christ, and allow them to judge it. Don't preach it or act on it until men of reputation who are seasoned in ministry have judged it first before you teach or preach it publicly. You don't want to run in vain. We should want our revelations and our ministries to be judged. Paul wanted this, and this is why he submitted his revelations to the apostles at Jerusalem who were well seasoned in ministry. All ministries must line up with the word of God. A true minister will teach sound doctrine. He will back up what he says with the word.

Old Testament prophets were the only ministry in operation from the standpoint of preaching or teaching the people. This is not true under the New Testament. Under the New Covenant, God has set the fivefold ministry in the church for the perfecting of the saints (Eph. 4:11-12 KJV). Under the New Covenant, every believer is to follow the Holy Spirit for himself. (Rom. 8:14 KJV) In the Old Testament God was dealing with the spiritually dead people; they couldn't worship God in spirit and in truth. Believers under the New Covenant are to worship God in spirit and in truth.

Under the old covenant, the Prophet (Holy Spirit upon him) gave guidance to the people because they didn't have the Holy Spirit for themselves. The people had to go to the Prophet to inquire what "thus, saith the Lord". Under the new covenant I believe the prophet and the pastor are the same. They are not in the office to lead or guide, but to teach God's word. Every believer has the Holy Spirit in them to help lead and guide. Each believer can hear from God without the help of a prophet (pastor). Therefore, under the new covenant, it is not scriptural to seek guidance from a prophet except for help in further understanding of God's word. Romans 8:14 (KJV) it says; "Sons of God can expect to be led by the Spirit of God". The number one way the Holy Spirit leads all Christians is by the inward witness. The Holy Spirit leads believers by the still, small voice, and believers are led by the authoritative voice of the Holy Ghost in their own spirit. These Pastors are only interested in winning mans souls for God. It's all about winning souls, not who has the biggest church or the most money etc.

I pray that this would happen in all churches and then maybe the Body of Christ (church) would start functioning the way it should, in balance and unity. Some would probably say to me, this is already happening, and I would say, please read 1Corintians 12 (KJV) and explain to me how the church is anywhere near unity in Christ. A minister once got upset with me and said I expected too much from him because his actions as a pastor didn't match what God's word says. I seen he was very upset so my answer to him was, I only expect from him what God's word says. If some of a pastors flock are carnal doesn't mean he should fall in step with them. Ministers should expect all Christians to follow the same guidelines as they do. A Pastors position is not something to take lightly. He is called by God to fill this position and he should be setting the Christian example. He is the Shepherd of the flock and shouldn't need anyone to explain his duties to him. It's all explained in His word. His position is more important then the President of any country. A pastor should be making sure his teaching of Gods word is absolutely true to protect his flock from the enemy.

A pastor needs to be a shepherd of the flock, protect it, teach them God's word, send them out to set the example that Jesus Christ set. A Pastor shouldn't be passive and only tell people what they want to hear, a watered down Gospel. Teach them the truth and let the Holy Spirit deal with the conviction. It says in James 3:1 (Amplified), "Not many [of you] should become teachers (self-constituted censors, and reprovers of others), my brethren, for you know that we [teachers] will be judged by a higher standard and with great severity [then other people; thus, we assume the greater accountability and the more condemnation]. James was concerned about man and his tongue. You know the uncontrollable tongue that continues to be out of control. If you can't control your tongue, my advice is for you to put it under the blood of Jesus, and if that don't work for you, pick another profession because you don't belong in a pastor or teacher position in a church. These positions are very important and God needs people that represent Him to show restraint especially if their in a position to judge and rebuke others. If you want approval from God, study his word and meet His standards. If preachers/teachers are not meeting the higher standard they need to take another look at God's qualifications and be prepared on the Day of Judgment. GOD SAID IT, I DIDN'T.

I remember sharing some scriptures God was showing me about a specific doctrine with members of the leadership in a Pentecostal church. They agreed to allow me this opportunity. After making a presentation that I knew was not agreeable to their way of believing, I only ask one question. Question: Do you agree or disagree with what I presented? It was almost a unanimous yes, they agreed. One leader didn't quite agree with everything I said, so I asked if we could get together again and discuss it and they agreed to do that. After a few weeks went by I received some feedback from others in the church and was told by some, and by one leader that they disagreed with me on what I presented. One leader started spreading false rumors about what I shared.

The word was passed around that I didn't agree with the Pentecostal experience for Christians today. That was an outright untruth. This particular leader only heard what they wanted to hear and not the whole presentation. This is how most misinterpretations of God's word occurs, only believing how you interpret His word and not really listening to someone else and their interpretation. There was four other people listening and none of them came back to me and said they disagreed. I tried to explain to the one leader that she was not listening to what I was saying and she was taking what I said out of context. Apparently she was afraid to speak up and disagree after my presentation and went behind my back and told the wrong story to some in the congregation. I requested to present the subject again to the leadership and congregation, but the leadership never answered my request. I would hope other churches are not like this, but I have my doubts. They not only didn't answer my request, they never answered anymore request I made, and there were many. I even told them if I was wrong and they could show me using God's word I would apologize to them and the congregation. They never responded.

The real problem was they have been teaching this particular doctrine for many years and if changed it would become a huge embarrassment to them. Even though some agreed with me, they went behind my back and disagreed. Was this political as usual or just the way Christian leaders react to protect their positions? Going behind my back and not allowing me to defend myself made me an outcast to other people in the church that didn't understand who was telling the truth. Why would they agree and then disagree? This reminded me of secular politicians that agree with people to get elected and then after elected, disagree and do it their way. I do believe that man is in control of the church and not the Holy Spirit. Some crooked ministers and church leaders are always trying to cover up their crimes like crooked politicians. The subject I presented was the gift of tongues and I will share this in another chapter. You can study it, ask God for guidance, and decide whether it's the truth or not.

We should always want an interpretation of God's word to be judged and proven by His word. When done this way there are no question or criticism from others to whether it's true or not. Ministries must always tell the truth and true ministers of God will. All leaders in a ministry must defend what they say about God's word. If you can't prove it and defend it with the word, it's not true. There are many

Christians with their personal agenda that can put a spin on God's word the way they want it. If you're not praying and making sure you're up to speed on His word it will be easy to fool you. A minister should never be offended by any challenge about a doctrine that might be wrong. True Ministers in our churches today need to get on their knees and ask God for help and guidance. The church is starting to be overrun with secular politicians and intellectuals that think they know best because they understand God's word better then everyone else.

Not long ago, I ask a pastor and his wife if they could defend a specific Bible doctrine they believe and teach to other people, and the answer was no, they couldn't. These two Christians have been teaching this particular doctrine for over forty years and can't use God's word to verify it. Where is the calling, and where is the truth, and why would they be teaching a doctrine they could not prove. Where is the spirit of God in their lives? God is going to get fed up with these weak Christian teachers soon and I wouldn't want to be in their shoes when He does. God is loving and patient, but serious, and the people taking advantage by doing wrong will pay the price. In cults this is called mind control. Are they in a cult?

As young Christians we have a tendency to believe much of what we are taught. I remember people sharing with me about a minister that was teaching God's word. They said he was a true man of God and I could believe everything he said about God's word. So here is a man that said he was called by God, been through Bible College, Ordained by a main-line Denomination, and given the authority to be a

Pastor in a church. We the people expect him to teach and preach the truth, so we believe everything he says about God's word. I believe some Christian youth are gullible in believing leaders whether secular or Christian. As we grow as Christians in the Lord the Holy Spirit starts showing us the truth and we start questioning things that don't match with God's word. Some people are gullible enough to believe what ever a pastor says without testing him. He might be a true man of God but he is still human and humans make mistakes. As new Christians we get indoctrinated into church doctrines and never study God's word to determine whether the doctrines are true to His word, using the Holy Spirit as our guide. Sometimes our ego and pride get in the way. God's word says to test the prophets.

After all is said and done we must make a decision using His word to verify the truth. When someone shares with you something that God has shown them in His word, and it has never been taught in the church, it should be tested. I had a minister tell me that most ministers have very big egos and have a tough time agreeing with others when it comes to hearing something new about God's word that they haven't taught. Some ministers and elders might agree with you but refuse to teach the truth. Why? It is embarrassment to them for not seeing it during their prayer time and studies. Some will fear they might lose their jobs because it's against the doctrine of the denomination they serve under. Even non-denominational ministers might agree with you about what God has shown you but refuse to share this truth because it might be opposite of what they have been teaching for years. The reason I say this is, the several presentations about what God has showed me in the past few years and most ministers and elders I shared it with have agreed, but will not share it with other Christians. Maybe they won't share it because God didn't show them first. They might eventually share it with their followers and make it look like God gave them a revelation. I really believe they won't share it because they are afraid they will lose their job. This is called fear (sin).

A very close minister friend of mine shared what he said was a revelation from God about who committed the first sin, Adam or Eve. He said God gave him a revelation that Adam committed the first sin, not Eve. After a short discussion with him, I ask him to prove it to me by using God's word. He didn't want to at that time. Instead of debating and saying to him that all things of this nature should be proven by God's word, I said I would study the subject and then we would continue our discussion. I studied and shared with him what God showed me.

This material comes from the King James Version of God's word. I ask you to read this with an open mind and prayer, asking for the Holy Spirits guidance and truth.

ORIGINAL SIN

Creation all happened by the supernatural powers of one God; God the Father, God the Son, God the Holy Spirit (trinity). God had no set of laws for our first parents to follow. Everything was given to them by the Father. He gave them a free will to make decisions for themselves. They were sin free and had control over everything on the earth. God only gave them one command. They could eat of the fruit of all trees except one. This tree became a test for them because of the enemy, Lucifer. God new he would eventually temp the woman. He is in a battle with God for mans souls and will not stop until he is cast into hell where he belongs, forever.

There was a delicate balance between man and woman in the beginning and the fall caused this balance to fail and this is what we see in relationships and marriages today. I think this delicate balance has gotten worse over the years and now is the cause of a complete breakdown in relationships and the family. The balance was broken and this caused man to tyrannize the woman and the woman has attempted to dominate the man. Paul says in Eph. 5:21-23 (KJV), they both need transformation. I believe the woman sinned first but God held them both responsible (Gen. 3:14-19 KJV). The unity of man and woman would be strained by their struggle for domination between them. There are some feminine Christian factions that would like to see this minister prove his revelation to be factual, but, that won't happen.

What God did in Gen. 3:14-17 (KJV) was a good indication that woman committed sin first. It was how He handed out sins penalties. Satan first, woman (female) second, and man (male) last. All were charged.

The beginning

Genesis: Chapter 1-3 (KJV) is an overview in proper sequence of creation of the earth and ending with man. If we put God's word into context we will find the truth. I do not twist God's word to try and match it with how some want it to say.

Chapter 1: 26-28; (KJV) And God said, Let us make man in OUR image, after OUR likeness: (more than one) and let THEM (more than one) have dominion over the fish of the sea, and over the fowl of the air, and over the cattle, and over all the earth. So God created man in His own image, in the image of God created he him; male and female created he THEM (two). And God bless THEM (both), And God said unto THEM (both), be fruitful, and multiply, and replenish the earth, and subdue it: and have dominion over the fish of the sea, and over the fowl of the air, and over every living thing that moveth upon the earth. There is no suggestion of inferiority of the female to the male. There is no suggestion of her submission to his dominance. They are male and female together as a representation. In Gen.2:20-25 (KJV) he gave her a name (woman) that was equivalent with him. This makes them equal, a balanced relationship.

God said "make man in OUR image, after OUR likeness: and let THEM have dominion"? Did God want man to be like Him (Trinity)? He gave BOTH of THEM equal dominion over everything on earth.

The following scriptures explain His COMMAND compared to what He GAVE them. There is a difference between what He gave THEM with no strings attached and what He commanded THEM to not do (strings attached).

Genesis 2:17 (KJV) "The tree of knowledge of good and evil, thou shalt not eat of it: for the day that thou eatest thereof, thou shalt surely die" (sins penalty), Gen. 3:19 (KJV), spiritual death, Prov. 8:36 (KJV). God gave a command for testing their obedience. So the sin for breaking his command is disobedience. When God created Adam and the woman He did not make a "command" to THEM to take dominion, He "gave" THEM dominion. God didn't give THEM commands on everything in the garden. He only said they could eat of every tree but the tree of knowledge of good and evil, they could not eat.

Genesis 3:1-7 (KJV), It doesn't say Adam was there. It says the serpent approached the woman, (serpent as in agent) and spent time with the woman. Prior to speaking to satan she knew God's command, whether straight from God or Adam makes no difference. In Gen. 3: 2-3 (KJV), the woman repeated what God said. Both Adams knew God and they walked and talked with Him in the Garden. Satan beguiled her and convinced her she would not die. The woman also added words that God did not say (neither shall ye touch it) which was a lie. Satan tells her, "ye shall be as gods, knowing good and evil." Genesis 3:6 (KJV) says, "And when the woman saw that the tree was good for food, and that it was pleasant to the eyes, and a tree to be desired to make them wise, she took of the fruit thereof, and did eat, and gave also unto her husband with her, and he did eat."

Genesis 3:8 (KJV), THEY heard the voice of the Lord God walking in the Garden in the cool of the day. Note: at this time, Adam had not given his wife a name, they were both

Adam. Verse 10, the guilt was there, God's word became fact. The conscience was born. In v20 it says "And Adam called his wife's name Eve; because she was the mother of all living. The question is who sinned first, Adam or Eve? In Gen. 1:26 (KJV), let THEM have dominion over everything upon the earth. This would mean THEY were equal partners. If only Adam was in charge and only he had dominion, why didn't he remove satan from the Garden? They both had dominion and I believe Eve could have removed satan, but chose not to. Why? They would be gods.

Remember, the sin was being disobedient to God, not being thy brother's keeper, which we know we're not. Genesis 3:12-14 (KJV) were all excuses by Adam and his wife for being disobedient. They could not accept their own guilt. This same type of blame shifting is still going on today.

Adam was created first and was allowed to name the animals. God then created a woman as a helpmate. Scriptures say God gave THEM dominion over everything on the earth. Both of them were made pure in the image of God. Nowhere does it say before the fall that Adam (male) was more important, had authority over the other Adam (woman) or that she was his subordinate. Some might say that the woman's name was still Adam (female) before the fall and this makes Adam sin first, but it was still the female Adam. Remember, this was all before the fall. Adam didn't have authority over the woman until after the fall. Authority over the woman started in Genesis 3:16 (KJV) when God penalized the woman for being disobedient when He said, "he will rule over you."

SIN'S PENALTY

Genesis 3:15-17 (KJV) God penalizes satan first, woman second, and Adam last.

Questions:

1. If Adam (male) was in charge of the Garden and should have known of satan's presence and was responsible for what happened to his wife, which would make him sin first for allowing it, why was he not penalized first and her second? God usually holds people in charge more responsible.

2. If Adam's wife was not equal with him before the fall, how come after the fall in Genesis 3:16 (KJV), God says, "thy desire shall be to thy husband and he shall rule over thee?" This sounds like a step down, a demotion in equal dominion with her husband. He will rule over you indicates that he did not have rule over her prior to the fall.

3. Do you think the woman had a desire to become a god as satan said before Adam to have the upper hand? God did create them in His own image, "in the image of God created He him; male and female He created He them" (Gen. 1:27 KJV). They both have dominion over the earth. God gave Adam a helpmeet to be his equal helper as God was his superior helper and the animals were his inferior helpers. Is this where desire to rule over others came into existence? Ref. Gen. 4:7.

4. If Adam did commit the sin first, please explain it, and where is it found in scripture?

Comment: God's word doesn't say anything about Adam knowing or being responsible for the woman's actions before the fall. Remember what God says about Cain and Abel not being each other's keeper. I believe after the fall the authority was given to Adam to guide his family and not lord over them. God still requires each person to make their own decisions. Eve did not become Adam's puppet, she is still his wife and looks for his guidance because God placed him head of the family. Why? Because Adam (male) did not commit the first sin, so God took the stronger of the two and made him responsible. Remember who satan approached first, woman. Now her obedience to him is just as important as our obedience to God. Children should be given the same guidance from their father and mother and receive the same obedience from them to God and parents.

Over the years we all have learned that study is important for our intellect and getting ahead in life. Some have to study more than others but we all have to study to get along in our society. My jobs over the years allowed me to work with many people holding degrees in chemistry, chemical and mechanical engineering, business, metallurgy, and many more. I found there were some very intelligent people, but there were some that couldn't see the trees for the forest if they tried (my opinion). I could share some stories about these well educated people that would blow your mind, but not now. As I've said in some of my statements that I believe in education, but how you get that education and how you use it is important. To study just enough to get passing grades in college is like some ministers of the Bible do to get ordained or get a degree in Bible theology. Once they get ordained or their degree, the study slows down, unless it's needed for their teaching each week. Some ministers have put together many sermons, keep them in a file, and then use them for teaching the people. This system is great as long as they are asking God what He wants the people to hear that particular day. I believe man has decided what people need and should hear, not God. Where does the Holy Spirit come in? I believe God decided the Holy Spirit should be in control, not man. If a minister does not have time during the week to pray and ask God what He wants the people to hear, but instead relies on a canned sermon, he should check his calling.

Remember God's word was given for us to read, and study, and understand how He wants us to live our lives. We should not be waiting for a minister to tell us how to live. The Bible is full of things about our past and tells us about our future. The Bible was not written, to be left on a table, and collect dust, or carry to church each Sunday for show. I've learned over the years when reading His word once, I thought I understood it until I read it again and again, and found out I really didn't understand it the first time. We need to read, study, and ask the Holy Spirit to guide and help us put everything into context. If we want the truth, read His word, study it, to prove it. Don't move to the left or right, keep your eyes and mind too the center, stay balanced. The church is full of unbalanced Christians that keep it splintered in all directions.

If we Christians (all people who have accepted the Lord as their savior) believe what it says in 1Cor.12 (KJV) about the Body of Christ, we should be working very diligently towards studying and discussing our differences and conclude, in agreement, using God's word to settle it. In order for this to happen we must be serious about our walk with God and put aside our differences in what we have been taught about specific doctrines. Most doctrines are taught to people without them reading or studying them to decide whether they are true or not. We accept them for many reasons. Such as, I really like the people and person explaining the doctrine, or this sounds good to me because this is what and how I want to believe, or this doctrine helps me and is opposite of all other doctrines, or this doctrine must be right because it doesn't have any self conviction in it and that is what I like about it. I could go on and on about why people like certain doctrines and not others. Just look at all the different denominations and their different doctrines.

The town where I grew up has a population of about 7-8 thousand, and there are about twenty five churches. What does this say about our differences and lack of understanding each other? Most of the churches have been there for many years and some are fairly new. What I observed while growing up was most of them were full of people on Sundays. If you visited these churches today you would probably see a small mixture of each ethnic group while most of the churches are still segregated. Among these twenty five churches there are Presbyterian, Lutheran, Catholic, Pentecostal, Methodist, Baptist and independent non- denominational. I don't have a count of how many people go to church each week so let us take a guess. There is an average of about fifty people that go to each church (25x50=1250) and that might be an exaggeration. That is a waste of energy, money, and people time. I would suggest we tear down all 25 churches and build a large one that will handle 2-4 thousand people. Everyone would meet in unity under one doctrine and the church will be integrated with all ethnic groups. The church could have multiple ministers. Each minister would take their turn ministering. If we don't do this and churches are continuing to be built, we Christians will eventually be attending a church with about five to ten people each Sunday and asking the question, where did everyone go? Some people would say this wouldn't work because of our different beliefs concerning God's word. I would say to them, don't underestimate the Creator. We might be surprised if we would just sit down and talk about our differences. There might not be many to overcome between Christians that really want to see unity in the body of Christ.

I had a conversation with a local minister of a large denomination about this subject. I explained to him, that years ago it was necessary for churches to be built in and around small communities, because of the lack of transportation. In our society today transportation is not a problem. Most families have their own transportation, so instead of building many small churches, we should build a few large churches in strategic areas. Each church would have two to three ministers, taking turns teaching and preaching. His response was, that would not work because he and most ministers have big egos and would not share a church. Guess what, that same ministers took a position in another church doing the same thing he said he wouldn't do. He is sharing a ministry with other ministers. Another problem is most denominational leaders are proud and bragging about how many churches they have built. God doesn't care about how many churches you build and how many people you bring in, He cares about how many souls you have won for Him. It's all about winning souls. Remember the war going on between God and Lucifer. We need get our eyes on the right target.

The bottom line for Christians is to consistently study God's word. If we want unity in the body of Christ Christians must talk and discuss with each other our differences. This means Pentecostals, Baptist, Methodist, Catholic, and all other Christian churches that believe there is one God. His Son died to save the world from their sins and sent His Holy Spirit to comfort and guide us. I could continue to tell stories about why we should study, study, study God's word but I believe you all understand. If you don't believe it let me ask this question. If all denominations say they are right in their doctrine, which one is telling the truth because some are different. Their answer would be they are. Why would God give different interpretations to the same scriptures? This is very confusing and God is not a God of confusion. God is very straight forward when talking about being a teacher of His word as the following scriptures point out, His Spirit is the teacher. All of the following scriptures come from the (KJV).

Luke 12:12- "For the Holy Ghost shall teach you in the same hour what ye ought to say". John 14:26 "But the

Comforter, which is the Holy Ghost, whom the Father will send in my name, he shall teach you all things, and bring all things to your remembrance, whatever I have said to you". 1Cor. 2:13-"Which things also we speak, not in the words which man's wisdom teacheth, but which the Holy Ghost teacheth; comparing spiritual things with spiritual". John 2:27-"But the anointing which you have received from him abideth in you, and ye need not that any man teach you: but as the same anointing teacheth you of all things, and is truth, and is no lie, and even as it has taught you, ye shall abide in him".

I believe all these scriptures say God's spirit will instruct us in all things. I really believe the scriptures point out what I'm trying to say. His spirit abideth in us. If we all have the same spirit as Christians, we should all be hearing the same words from God the Father. God's spirit tells the truth and does not lie. So, if we are living under doctrines that are different from what God's word says we are living a lie. So who is telling a lie? Them, him, her!!! Not me! Who?

CHAPTER FOUR

WHAT HAPPENED TO THE CHURCH, (THE BODY OF CHRIST)?

What I have to say in this chapter is an opinion about churches that I have attended based on my observations over the years and having discussions with other Christians attending different denominational churches. This also happens in other denominational churches. In the 1990'S my family and I were very surprised when we visited a church after a time of absence. We were always use to the church being full of people and now there was only a hand full. We started asking questions about the lack of people attending and never got a straight answer from anyone including all the leadership and the pastor. It appeared that most small churches in the area were having the same problem so I decided I would spend some time trying to find out why and share with everyone my analysis.

I'll tell you why my family and I stopped going to church in the eighties. It was because of the politics being played and ministers and elders accepting it and most of the members not recognizing the problem. It become a contest of personalities and more about control of the church organization by man then it did about worshiping God. It has slowly become a Christian society loaded with hypocrisy that caused some Christians to lose faith and sinners not wanting to participate. In other words the church died spiritually because man wanted to take control. In the last Pentecostal church we attended, the services were more like a sporting event then a church service. I observed what God was showing me about fakes in the church over the years but these services were over the top when it came to pushing the secular way and not God's way of doing things, allowing the Holy Spirit to have control. I guess some might ask the question, why didn't you and your family buck the system and get rid of the politicians? We tried and suffered ridicule by other Christians. My family was better off, not being put through all the negatives caused by outright lies by Christian leadership that were blind to what was going on.

Then because of our secular society changing in how to deal with the youth, the church fell right in line and followed suit. The church was sucked into the secular way of doing things. Examples: how to raise your children, give them everything they want including all the new electronics, let them stay in their rooms to play with all these new gadgets and not get any exercise (obesity), play all the sports from the time they are old enough and tell them how great they are, even if they aren't (the self-esteem problem?), and change the laws in the schools so teachers have a tough time with discipline. I could go on, but I believe you see what I mean. So here comes a different group of people, mostly young that are all about themselves. The youth today want to take control and become the leaders, but taking control because they feel they can do a better job is not what it's all about. If it is done God's way and not the secular way it will work. Some churches have failed to teach young people what Jesus taught His disciples and that was to share the gospel, and if you have a calling on your life from God move out into the ministry. If God calls you to a specific ministry, stick with it. The church felt if they didn't start using the youth they would completely lose them. This is what the church has become. We have spoiled our youth by catering to them and today they believe they should have control. It's called satisfying their ego and building their self-esteem. In other words it's all about me.

On April 17, 2010 I read an article written by J. Lee Grady concerning the Pentecostal movement. It was about a New Generation Embracing the Holy Spirit's Fire. This took place at a conference called Empowered 21 in Tulsa at the ORU campus. There were many Pentecostal organizations present. It was a very impressive showing of the Pentecostal movement in this country. It was ironic that I would receive this information at this time because I had already written about the Pentecostal church and the youth problem. I read as much of Mr. Grady's material as I can because I believe he is trying very hard to make sure the truth is being told, although I believe this article is somewhat misleading. I still believe he is going in the right direction when it comes to the truth about God's word. I pray that he don't get coned by any evil doers.

He says the purpose of the conference was to bridge the generation gap and call younger Christians to take responsibility for the future of the charismatic renewal. I have attended Pentecostal churches for many years and seen changes in how Pentecostals have cooled spiritually, drop off in attendance, political church splits, ministers with fear of losing their position, thieves in some leadership positions, ministers lacking the call from God, and ministers not fulfilling their original call by God by taking a different position in the ministry. This is another indication that man is making the decisions, not God. You name it, I've seen it. The Pentecostal church is in trouble with the youth or they would not have had this conference. I would like to say I believe most churches are having trouble keeping the youth active in their churches and for many reasons. In this book I talk about why the youth have slowly steered clear of the church in the past twenty to thirty years. I just recently ask four ministers what happened to all the youth. Their answer given to me was, they didn't know.

From the 1980's to 2012 there has been a breakdown in teaching in the church that has caused a separation between the youth and elders. What has caused this? My wife and I were completely stunned by the change. We were always use to participating with the youth and the unity was always there. We were completely surprised to see and hear a minister teach separation of young and old in a church we attended. I could relate many stories about lay witness missions during the Seventies with the youth and how successful they were.

There was no wall between the young and old. These missions were held in different churches and the people of other denominational backgrounds participated. Today young people want to take control and lead everything and because the church needs them, ministers fall for this con. The youth need this because society has failed them and their self-esteem needs attention. They need an ego builder and this is where they get it from. Ministers are allowing the youth to lead, not knowing there background or even if they are Christians. Some young Christians will talk about God one minute and use foul language the next minute. They do this in God's sanctuary and I believe some ministers do this also and they are leading the church.

We humans never want to go to the root cause of the problem. No one wants to stand up and take the blame and say we caused the problem. I believe hypocrisy is one and probably the root cause of the church problems yesterday and today. The other is the lack of truth which is not being taught. Why can't Christians stand up and be accounted for and tell the truth. If we want to represent God the Father in truth this would be a good start. Maybe there wouldn't be so many different denominations if the truth was told. First we humans would have to do away with our egos, self-esteem, pride, and then repent again and humble ourselves before God, be honest and ask Him to help us understand His truth. What a huge step that would be for most Christians. Before getting into my reasons why I believe the church has failed I would like to ask some questions. We all need to ask ourselves these questions and answer them honestly. You know, tell the truth.

SAMUEL D. SCULL

Question: What is your opinion to why people stop attending church? May I ask the following to help us come to a conclusion?

Are people just tired of playing church? Do I go because it's a habit or just a social gathering? Do I go because I am political minded and find the church a place to show my political skills? Do I only go for hand outs because it's tough times? Do I go because I like the way the church looks inside and outside? Do I go because the minister favors me more than others? Do I go because I am looking for a mate? Do I go just to be seen? Do I go because my parents and other family members go? Do I go just because my spouse goes? Do I go because the church doctrine is the way I want to believe? Do I go because if I do things out of order and wrong, I never get challenged? Do I go because people in the church hold me in high esteem as a leader? Do I go because I am in the inner circle with the pastor? Do I go because I am on the church board? Do I go because intellectually I am smarter then everyone else and the minister will pick me to be #2? Do I go because I can quote more scriptures than anyone in the church and this puts me in a position to become a teacher?

Would I go if I was not on the board or in the inner circle? Do I go because I have been taught my church doctrine is the only one that is true according to the Bible? Did I ever read and study the background of the church I attend? Did I ever try to prove by using the Bible whether the church doctrine where I attend is true or false? Do I go because I am getting a kick back from all the money being taken in? Do I go just to please someone? Last but not least, do I go because I want to fellowship with other Christians and worship God and learn about his word?

I'm not saying people don't worship God when in church, I'm saying all of the above questions need to be answered to determine how serious we are about God. If we're serious we need to get rid of all the other stuff that hinders the church from moving ahead. I could go on and on with other questions, but I think these are enough to show Christians have many reasons why they attend church. If you answer all these questions truthfully you might find out, some Christian only play church. The problem with these type questions is it becomes very difficult for people to give honest answers. It would be admitting the truth and that would be embarrassing. Were we being honest when ask the question, would you like to receive Jesus Christ as your savior or was it just a political answer? Some people are not serious about following God's standards for themselves and building the true body of Christ. The question we all need to ask ourselves is, do I really have the new man in me? It's all about being born again with our spirit joined to God's spirit which is the power we need to live a strong Christian life.

Church attendance cycles up and down and could be caused by many things. One could be external problems around the world. If there are wars, famines, disasters (earth quakes, volcano eruptions, etc) and it affects peoples lives church attendance increases. Why? When the human race gets their back against the wall they start looking to God for help, and when everything is okay they take control back and forget about God. Why? They got what they wanted from God and now they can go back to there way of living. During the first half of the 20ᵗʰ Century the country had two wars, went through a depression, earthquakes, dust bowls in the west, and the San Francisco fires. There were plenty of people in church. During the second half of the Century we had two more wars, catastrophic earthquakes, volcano eruptions, bad hurricanes etc, and the churches were still full. In the last quarter of the 20ᵗʰ Century the churches started to loose people. This is when things were looking very good for everyone. This is the way they lived their lives all through the Old Testament. Another reason could be caused by internal problems in the church (body of Christ). Protestant and Catholic churches have had their internal problems that caused a drop in attendance over the years caused by hypocrisy and lies. Satan is still at war with Christians to win converts over to his way of thinking. Satan has never stopped waging war with the church, families, and government. He is slowly breaking them down. Our government was founded by Christians who put God first and now they are trying to remove Him.

All Christians must put God first, but today we are slowly putting Him last by not teaching the whole truth. Some ministers pick and choose which scriptures people should hear. They are afraid to tell the whole story because of backlash from their followers. Some people only want to hear what they consider necessary to help them build their self-esteem. Some scriptures might convict them so certain scriptures are removed from all sermons. What they really want is to do away with God's conviction and the conscience. They want no conviction and they want to live in a no-fault world. Some families are being destroyed because of new laws allowing divorce for any reason. Married couples are not under any pressure to try and make a marriage work when all they have to do is hire a lawyer, file the paperwork, and wait for a period of time. I know there are circumstances when people should get a divorce and I believe God's word teaches that. I've seen times in the past when everything was okay and the churches didn't have any problem with attendance. I believe this was during a time when evangelism had exploded in this country and around the world and about twenty years ago it stopped. Why? Ask the ministers in the churches. Good luck!!!

Some Christian organizations around the world have been concerned about the exodus of people from churches in this country. I was sharing this with a local minister, praying he would understand the problem the American Christian church is having. I shared with him that I believed most churches have left the Holy Spirit outside and allowed the political man to stay inside and take control. Ministers around the world are concerned and are saying the same thing. The minister got upset with me and said, he really didn't care what the ministers around the world think, they were wrong. I believe this was self denial on his behalf. What he was saying is, only the ministers in this country know the truth, but when I ask what happened to all the people, his answer was he didn't know. He told some Christians during a Bible study at my residence that he was the only one in control at his church. I believe the pastor should oversee all activities at the church he is responsible for, if that is what he meant. What he forgot was the Holy Spirit is his guide and controls what should be done and how it should be done, not him. The Holy Spirit is our teacher, He guides in all truth, He controls the movement of believers, He directs the selection of all Christian leaders, He chooses the field of operation, He is called the Spirit of Truth, and He is our Comforter. He is God's power here on earth.

To say you are in control and not the Holy Spirit is coming close to blasphemy. I honestly believe that many Christian ministers today believe alike. They are in control and not the Holy Spirit, and I believe this is one of the key reasons why most churches are failing. What I mean by failing is there are very few people in their churches and hardly any new souls won by those attending. Some ministers will even admit they were dismissed from one church and moved to another church because they failed to grow the membership. After about five churches they are put on notice and given one more chance. Out of frustration they start using secular gimmicks to increase membership because they fail to listen to the Holy Spirit as their guide. When the pastor sends his report to Denominational Headquarters it looks good on his part and he takes the credit, saving his job. Not much is ever said about saving souls, it was all about growing membership. Why would a mainline denomination leave someone in a Pastor role that couldn't make it in any church he was assigned to? It might be called "all in the family". Only God draws men unto Himself. These type ministers will play this game until they get what they want and where they want to be. Most of the people at the Bible study were upset with his statement and some of them were members of the church where he was Pastor. Not enough emphasis is put on salvation, and too much emphasis is put on church growth, and greed (money), which is causing some people to leave the church.

I listened to a teaching on who is in control, God or man, by an excellent teaching minister. His whole teaching was about God being in control. I agree!! The only problem I have with just saying God is in control is, God will not take back what he gives and commands. When God created man He gave them dominion (control) over the earth and everything in it. This means God gave them authority to rule over everything on earth. When satan showed up in the garden our first parents new they were in control. God was still present, but He allowed them to control their own future. He only gave them one command and it had a consequence attached. He said if you violate this command you will surely die, (meaning spiritually).

God let them know up front that His command was serious and if violated the consequence was the end of their control of everything on earth. This meant they could no longer talk or fellowship with God. After the fall God still wanted a relationship with His creation and continued looking for men who would be obedient to Him. In the Old Testament God chose who He wanted to communicate with and put His Holy Spirit upon. I know God's grace covers much, but it does not eliminate his laws and commands. God's Day of Judgment will happen. After the fall we became spiritually dead, and not on speaking terms with God and because of what His Son did for us it opened the line of communication again with the Father for all who believed in Him, because of His Grace. His Son is our attorney and goes before the father on our behalf.

He gives authority to a pastor to oversee all functions in the church. He gave man a mind of his own and a free will. God did not control mans decision to sin and it surely wasn't satan, it was man. Man controls his own destiny, not God or satan. If this is not true than why did God give us a choice, heaven or hell, and we must make that decision. God did this because He gave only one command to our first parents and they decided to disobey. I believe God is in control of what He said in His Word and He will control everything forever. We give to much credit to satan when we do things wrong. We must remember he has no control over what we do. He can influence us by deception as he did to our first parents but he can't control us. Remember satan could not deceive Jesus, so if we have Jesus in us and are serious he cannot deceive us. If we do wrong it is because we want to. Satan loves it, but didn't cause it.

A minister told me when I started attending his Bible study group at his house that all the people wanted to talk about was vacation, boats and fishing, but never about God. He told me he was glad that I started attending and brought God into the conversation. I was really concerned why he didn't insist on talking about God himself, that is what a Bible study is for. I felt greed was the problem. I thought Christian interest should be about what Jesus would want and then follow in his footsteps. It should be about sharing our testimony and let God provide all our needs according to His will. The problem with man taking control is everything he wants and gets becomes an idol to him.

The sins of jealousy and greed are also playing a large roll in church problems. You know the old saying, "I want everything the Jones' have, home, boat, cars, good job, money etc." We Christians take our eyes off of what God wants for us and put our eyes on what the world has. Our secular world has always been and always will be a want, want, greedy society. Christians always fall into the same sin driven system as the secular society. Most Christians today are striving for the same things the rest of the world has. This is one of the main problems the United States has with the rest of the world. They are jealous of everything we have in this country and they want it. I know they would all like the freedom we have, and I can't blame them. In 2010 our liberal Government wants everyone to share the wealth. This is the socialist way of doing things. My wife and I recently spent two weeks in France and it amazed me to see so many people just setting around tables on the sidewalks doing nothing but chatting with each other. I soon found out the government was paying them not to work. The people who were working and paying their taxes were sharing the wealth so these people could just relax and do their thing. I've seen some of that same thing in this country for the past sixty years.

False doctrine is another problem in our Christian society that causes people to leave the church. There are some denominational doctrines that are very controversial. One problem in our Christian society is we all believe the church we attend has the true answer and the right interpretation of all of God's word. No one ever wants to meet and seriously discuss their differences. This is how the

Christian intellectual sees it, I'm right and you're wrong (not a spiritual answer), it is always mans opinion. There never is any discussion. So, for the sake of argument let's use the Gifts God gave us in 1Cor. 12. Not all Christians believe they are for today. Why? I can't read any scripture where it says it was only for people back in Jesus' time. We Christians should be using these gifts to determine why the church needs help.

I recall going through some Bible College material and came across this phrase "if you don't obey you can't pray". After thinking about this phrase for awhile I started studying more about prayer and the reason why this was put in the college material. After some study I ended up agreeing with the statement. When sharing this with one of the instructors and two ministers they disagreed with the statement immediately without any thought or discussion, even though they had read it many times during their teaching. They said they would have it removed. Because they disagreed with the statement I was wrong for agreeing with it along with the one who wrote it. The instructor and ministers were correct without any discussion to make sure whether it was a true statement or not. They didn't ask me why I believed it or give me a chance to share why. There was no explanation why I was wrong and they were right, except they were the leaders and in control. This is one of the main reasons why we have so many different denomination and non-denominational churches. Christians have a very difficult time agreeing with each other. They are still using mans thinking and not God's knowledge and wisdom from His Holy Spirit to make decisions about the word. They are not asking the Holy Spirit for His guidance in these matters. Man is still in the same mind thought as our first parents were by not stopping and asking God for guidance before acting on it.

There are many other doctrines in different churches that need to be shared and discussed of a similar nature, but no one wants to sit down and discuss them. So people go through life not knowing the truth and maybe believing a false doctrine. All I wanted was an open discussion and an understanding why they disagreed, using God's word. This is how it should be done.

When reading and studying the history of the Christian movement over the years, one must ask the question, why did man take the Christian church to the political arena in this country and around the world or was it always this way? Then I remembered God gave man a will of his own. Man has used his will and intellect over the years to take control of not only the church but also peoples lives, and will continue to have control until Christ second coming unless he humbles himself and ask forgiveness. Adam and Eve took control for man in the Garden when not adhering to God's command and committing the first sin. Man still had control when Jesus was here on earth and has control today over his own destiny. Man needs to return control, allowing God's Holy Spirit to do His work, to guide and comfort. Just think, if we would all ask God for guidance in our lives and listen to what He says, we would all be in a better place and maybe this world would not be like it is today.

We still have many freedoms in this country unlike most of the world because of our constitution which was written by people who believed in God and prayed before their meetings, asking Him for guidance. That is what this country was all about, people wanting to be free and worship God in freedom. They wanted a country built around Christian values. After sending many missionaries in past years from this country to other countries around the world, the other countries are now starting to ask us not to send them anymore. They are saying they would rather send their missionaries to the United States. Why? They say Christians in the U.S. have lost touch with God by not allowing His Holy Spirit to control our lives and church services. If man humbles himself before God and ask forgiveness, and then allows the Holy Spirit to guide him, things will change.

Because of non-believers and other religious belief systems in this country our government is starting to interpret our constitution different than the framers. They are slowly doing away with our Christian way of living by allowing people from other countries to gain citizenship or even being illegal aliens to concentrate on doing away with everything having to do with our God. The secular society with their leader (satan) is slowly deceiving the Christian society into believing everything is okay, just follow along and become a society of lazy believers. We became a strong Christian country because of our Christian beliefs and now our government allows the minorities, such as the atheist, Islam, and other none Christian groups to slowly eliminate God. Because of this we are becoming a weaker nation.

What we allow to happen in this country will sooner or later happen in other Christian countries. It's like a cancer, slowly destroying everything we believe in, from the inside out, until we all lose our religious freedom.

Do we know what the constitution says about our freedoms? If we were born in this country and don't know, shame on us. I am one who will admit that I don't know as much as I should about it and I was born here. We have become a country of people who take everything for granted. You know how some believe, everything will be okay, don't worry. We have become so lazy about what is really happening around us, especially with our government and church we will eventually lose everything that our forefathers fought for. In some cases it makes no difference whether we care or not, because the two political parties have gone astray and stopped representing the people. We elect these people to represent us and when they get in office they forget about us and only think about themselves and their political party. Our government has become so corrupt it will take a miracle to straighten it out. Maybe if we all start praying God will set a fire under all their chairs. This would keep them on their feet and open their eyes to the damage they are causing in our country. We elect these people and expect them to do what they say. We are supposed to trust them, but we forget they are just like our first parents who made a wrong decision that affected all mankind. Man has never learned his lesson.

The same goes for the Bible in respect to understanding what it says and not someone telling you what it says and means. I will also admit while growing up, attending church, I took the word of the ministers as gospel (truth). We are not living in times when you would be put to death for even having a Bible in you possession. This still might happen in some countries around the world but not in this country, as of yet. If we believe in God and the Bible is His written Word, we need to study it and put things into proper context for ourselves. After doing so, compare it with things happening around the world today especially in the church (the body of Christ). As I've said ministers around the world say they don't want the Christian church in the United States to continue sending missionaries. Why? Because they believe Christians in this country have slowly moved the Holy Spirit out of the churches and their lives, and now are letting man take His place as comforter and guide. In other words man has taken the control away from God's spirit.

Everyone in this country has the freedom of religion and they are free to defend their religion in a peaceful way. There are many countries around the world that will not allow this. But we the people in this country must follow the laws even if it doesn't meet our religious beliefs. We don't have to bow down to any leader, but we must abide by the laws. Jesus obeyed the law by paying the taxes and He didn't have to. Kings and their families didn't pay taxes, so Jesus, being a King was free to not pay, but instructed Peter to do so, as not to offend. Our Judicial system needs to be just and fair when it comes to deciding cases or complaints, not allowing one religious group to take advantage of another. I have seen some disparities in some resent court decisions when it comes to Christianity and Islam. This nation was founded on Christian beliefs and has been a Christian nation ever sense. Our President today says we are no longer a Christian Nation. Why? I would guess it's because of his background or the Islam religious group in this country has persuaded him to do so, or for political reason. This is another indication of where we are being lead as a nation, away from our Christian values and beliefs. Using religious statements like this to get votes doesn't seem ethical. But what is ethical about our Government anyhow?

We have laws in this country and we are supposed to abide by them. I believe most Americans do abide by the law but there are a few that could care less. There are thieves, murderers, and many more that continually violate the laws. Some are legally punished and some get away with their crimes. There are some laws that are overlooked by our appointed and elected officials and nothing is ever done to correct these violations. If I violated one I would probably be locked up. There are about twelve million Mexicans violating an immigration law and for many years our government leaders have let them violate this law. I believe it is about time we citizens insist these laws be adhered to or let everyone break all the laws they want and do nothing to them. I believe this is called anarchy. If some can break the law, why not let all? Maybe the President would give amnesty to all law breakers. Politicians will always say this didn't start on my watch. It might not have started on their watch, but it should stop when their watch started. Now that it has lasted so long liberal politicians will use twelve million Mexicans as pawns for their political advantage. I could continue expressing my thoughts about our judicial system in this country, but it will be a waste of my time.

I just recently read an eight page booklet called "The Prayer Room in the United States Capitol". This booklet was printed in 1956 and sense I don't visit the Capitol I'm not sure the prayer room is still there. Anyhow on page one it says "Near the Rotunda of the Capitol there is a room set apart for prayer. It is not a room for religious assemblies or for any other public use. Its only use is to provide a quiet place to which individual Senators and Representatives may withdraw a while to seek Divine strength and guidance, both in public affairs and in their own personal concerns." Fifty plus years have passed sense this room was made available to everyone in Congress. I wonder how many Representatives and Senators take time today to visit this important place to pray. It's hard to believe that just over fifty years ago people that were elected to Congress still had similar thoughts that the framers had, and that was God was still in control. They needed a place to be alone while they prayed to God for advice about our country and the path it was taking.

These are partial quotes from the booklet. "A reverent simplicity pervades the room. Ordinarily, the lighting is subdued, yet sufficient to direct attention to the two central objects—a Bible, opened to the twenty third Psalm, and the window symbolizing our nation at prayer. A concealed ceiling light focuses upon the altar on which the open Bible rests. Members of Congress may use this Bible, turning to whatever great passage may mean the most to them at the moment.

The single window speaks of that religious faith which has always been a part of the greatness of our Nation. The central figure is of the kneeling Washington, reminding us of the words of his First Inaugural: "....it would be peculiarly improper to omit this first official act, my fervent supplication to that Almighty Being who rules over the Universe, who presides in the councils of nations, and whose providential aids can supply every human defect, that His benediction may consecrate to the liberties and happiness of the people of the United States, a Government instituted by themselves for these essential purposes, and may enable every instrument employed in its administration to execute with success the functions allotted to his charge."

In the medallion, immediately surrounding the central figure, woven in the ruby glass, is the text from Psalm 16:1, "Preserve me O God: for in Thee do I put my trust."

This is enough to show that people once trusted God and wanted Him in everything they did, even in our schools. Take God out and let who in? If this room is no longer available we should be ashamed. But as I said earlier in this chapter, we allow this to happen because we are leaving God out of all we do.

Many people of the world that want to come to this country that are waiting in line to become legal citizens, and even illegal immigrants probably know more about our constitution than the average citizen that was born here. We allow our elected politicians to write the laws and then appoint judges to interpret them. All of those people who wrote the constitution and sign the document in agreement had the people's best interest in mind. They were doing their job, representing the people. Our congress today can't agree on anything unless it's down party lines. No wonder the people are now considering a third party. The politicians mind set is, if it is not liberal or conservative forget about it. It becomes deadlock and nothing gets done. There is a light at the end of the tunnel, it's called independent. There are people getting tired of this two party system and hopefully will eventually break it up unless politicians decide to be honest and represent the people and not their party.

The politicians blame each other for the country being polarized when they know both political parties are responsible. Both parties have the voters where they want them, voting down party lines, not voting their conscience. Politicians and voters do not vote their conscience anymore. Power and greed is the name of the game, not serving the people who put them in office. I remember the vote in congress on whether to leave a President in office or remove him, and the media was asking the politicians how they would vote. Republicans and democrats pretty much all said they would vote their conscience. Guess what, they voted down party lines. I guess the party line is their conscience.

When politicians ask you to vote for him or her, ask them if they have a conscience and do they truthfully plan on representing the people and not themselves. If they say yes, tell them not to lie about it when voting on an important bill that affects the people. Tell them if they continue this party line game it will be their last time in office. In most cases it's not voting because you're a conservative or liberal, it's what you will gain or not gain for your vote. We all know it's about pork fat and I believe that should be considered bribery.

Politicians buy votes by passing bills that profit certain groups of people. When our politicians quit doing this, and start telling the truth, and show the people they are serious about representing all and not just a few, this country will return to being strong and a great example for the rest of the world. Our politicians and Judges put too much of their personal thoughts and feelings into making decisions for the people instead of doing their jobs according to what their responsibilities are. In other words, write the laws, abide by how they were written and understood when voted on. Our Supreme Court Judges are becoming more political then ever before. If the truth be known most decisions by Judges are probably made according to their political party affiliation. To politicians, it's all a chess game. They spend more of their time spending money and play this chess game instead of paying more attention to what the people really want, and doing the job they were elected for.

We would be well served if the politicians in Washington DC would start telling the truth, adhere to the laws, quit being so greedy, stop stealing from the people, and vote on bills that don't have pork fat. Our representatives in Congress don't read most of the bills that comes before them, and they look at how much pork they will get if they vote for it. This should be called bribery from both sides. I have always felt that many of them are crooks, but now I truly believe most of them are. I believe most of our politicians are lawyers and they are always looking for loopholes in a bill after they are passed instead of making sure the loopholes are not there before it's passed. This is so far from representing the people, it's not funny. I guess like some have said we need to throw them all out of office and start over, but the young people working for these politicians today are being taught all their bad habits.

What I'm trying to show here is the comparison of the secular world to the Christian world. Our Government is starting to leave God out of all things and the church is slowly doing the same thing. The secular government and Christian church are both political. Maybe we shouldn't elect people in either arena that aren't willing to do as our forefathers and that was to pray and ask God for guidance. If other religious groups don't appreciate our Christian walk let them go back to their own countries and do what they want the way they want to do it. Christians need to pray for this Country, and the Government, and ask God to show them the path they are taking is the wrong one.

CHAPTER FIVE

THE MODERN CHURCH ("BODY OF CHRIST")

The church is changing and I believe all Christians should question the changes. As I've said in chapter two the churches have lost many people to the secular way of living and gained very few new converts. This looks like satan is winning a battle for some souls. Ministers that I've spoken with say they don't know what happened to all the people. Some say it's a cycle the church goes through and I agree. It is either hot or cold and when you average out hot and cold it becomes lukewarm. The cycle is there for many reasons and the church leadership refuses to address it. If someone leaves the church and you ask the pastor or any leader what caused them to leave the stock answer is they don't know. We Christians watch the attendance in church drop, some are concerned, and some aren't, but we do nothing about it. There is always a war going on between layman and leadership. It becomes a blame game. It usually ends up a disaster because we blame each other for causing it. We continue to say that's just the way it happens. What we really need to say is we are too lazy and afraid to tackle the issue as long as some new people eventually replace a few of the ones that leave. Of course there are not enough converts to keep up with the losses, so the church ends up with a handful of people. I'll stick out my neck and say I believe the problem is Church politics that causes strife and confusion that eventually drives people away. This is caused from the top down and bottom up, and we recognize it, but don't want to do anything about it. Greed and hypocrisy are also leading factors in church problems.

Mega churches are now taking some of the people that leave the small churches. People around the country might not attend these churches, but watch them on TV or listen to them on the radio. They also support them with their tithes. This is a way of participating without getting involved in church wars. The only problem with some of the Mega churches is they aren't preaching the whole Gospel. The whole story needs to be told so Christians are balanced in there sharing of God's Word. Some of these ministers have developed a Christian "feel good society". Remember the song "Don't Worry Be Happy", this is the new church attitude, because nothing you do is wrong. If we have no conscience it means we have no conviction to deal with. All people worry about today is their self -esteem. I recommend everyone read John Macarthur's book on the Vanishing Conscience. He talks about drawing the line in a No-Fault, Guilt-Free World. It is one of my favorite books having to do with human behavior. God gave man a conscience and man is trying his best to get rid of it. Why? Because it interferes with his self-esteem, destroys his ego, and he can't deal with that. It's an attitude that's all about me!

Here is a list of some things that I believe causes people to leave their churches. These things will also destroy a church if not stopped. Answers to solve these problems are in Gods word. They also are some of the reasons why we have so many different denominations and no one ever wants to sit down and discuss the differences.

1. Politics: Families wanting to take over operation of the church, and other families don't like it so they leave. Intellectuals and others thinking they know how to do things better so give them control. People wanting a position or control because they think they are the only ones qualified. Some people with the "gift of gab" faking a prophet's (false prophet) roll. I believe politics is probably the main cause for church strife and division. Because of the political climate in the secular world today and how it has spilled over into the Christian world wanting to control everything, it is causing people to be dissatisfied and leave the church.

2. Fear and paranoia: Ministers (Pastors) always afraid someone is trying to take their position or the church away from them (they either have no calling or their faith is questionable). Pastors wanting things their way only, and not taking advice from anyone. It's the Pastors idea and not coming from God. Some Pastors will stunt the church growth with unnecessary fear and paranoia. If this type

leadership is not stopped it will completely destroy a church.

3. Strife: This is when people are not satisfied with leadership or vice-versa. There is discontentment about many things and no agreement on anything. Too many questions ask by laypeople and many never answered. Always butting heads with one another because God is never in the discussion. Most leadership believes strife is always caused by the layman and that is not true. When God is not included in our discussions it will cause strife in the church. This can be caused by anyone, including the leadership. Strife can be caused by many other things and most of the time it's never addressed by the leadership.

4. Hypocrisy: People wanting everyone to believe they are Holier than thou but really aren't, they are very good actors. Christians living on both sides of the fence. Any Christian professing to be walking the walk and talking the talk and continuing to live a life of sin. People judging other people using God's word, but need to look in the mirror at them selves. People interpreting the scriptures to fit their own beliefs and using those beliefs to control other people. People accusing others of sinning and using Matt.18 to address it, but are sinning themselves.

5. False doctrine: Ministers teaching or preaching a doctrine that can't be proven by God's word. Some believe the doctrine and some don't because God is not in the center of the discussion. False doctrine

has caused Christians to develop many different denominations over the years. With all the different denominations someone has to be teaching and preaching a false doctrine. The question is, who?

6. Cults: People who want to control people for their own benefit using false doctrine to do so. People that search out people that are easily convinced about a doctrine that will lead them down the wrong path. People who lead these groups are mentally sick and prey on people that are gullible. I also believe anyone who adds to or takes away from God's word (the Bible), meaning, if you have written your own bible, it's a cult.

7. Differences: Personalities, education, and social status. There never has been enough teaching on personality types to help us understand why people think and do things different. There are four distinct personalities. We all have one of them and an added mixture from four grandparents in each of us. Do you know which one you are? We think different and this is why there are liberals, conservatives, and independent thinking people in our government and churches, and might I add, so many different denominations. Our churches are loaded with different personalities. Some educated people believe because of their education they should be in control of everything. Education and money becomes a bearing on human social status. You know the old saying, "which side of the railroad tracks do you live on"? God is not a respecter of

persons. He looks at everyone as being equal. We might think we are better than others, but, we are not according to God.

8. Jezebel spirit: One who is full of pride, call themselves a prophet, very manipulative, spreads gossip, has a loose tongue and will admit it. This demon will destroy a church and continue with gossip, knowing it. They need psychological help and because of their religious beliefs will not admit it. They might move from church to church or stay as a permanent member in one church and continue their destructive ways, driving people away. A casting out of the demon would help.

9. Pride: Putting your human pride before God. In other words everything that comes out of your mouth is all about you, your spouse, and family. The people know more about you and your family than about God and His word. People with the jezebel spirit are usually full of human pride. They are always comparing themselves with others trying to prove that they and their family members have done better in everything and this becomes overbearing to others. It is okay to be proud of your accomplishments and your family, but to continually brag about them. God's word says this is a sin. In James 4:6 (KJV) it says, but now ye rejoice in your boastings: all such rejoicing is evil.

Along with reasons why people leave churches, here are some reasons why some Christians ruin their testimony about God and His word. We become hypocrites and this causes people to think twice about getting involved. This type of problem has caused the Christian church to become a place where some would not attend. You might say I'm crazy, but please put some prayer and thought in what I'm saying.

Some churches mislead the world with their doctrines. Pentecostals believe in the gift of speaking in tongues and by doing this means you are baptized in the Holy Spirit and other denominations disagree. Baptist believe in "once saved always saved", other Christian churches disagree. Some Catholics believe in worshiping the Mother Mary, all Protestant churches disagree. We need to take a good look at all these scriptures and not be afraid to openly discuss them. Because there are so many different interpretations of what God's word says it becomes very difficult for people to decide who is right or who is wrong. God's word is not that complicated. The gifts are in God's word and speaking in other tongues is one of them. I can't find anywhere in God's word where it says you have to speak in tongues to be baptized in the Spirit. I can read nothing about the mother of Jesus being elevated to the level of worship by others. The Catholic Church needs to tell the whole story of why they elevated her to be equal in status with Jesus back in the fourteenth/fifteenth centuries. The reason is available in most religious history books. Once saved, always saved is another subject I would like to discuss with the Baptist so we Christians being part of the body of Christ would understand how they come to this conclusion.

Some ministers teach and preach healing, but have a tough time with being healed themselves. Examples: Some ministers I knew in the past and some I know now had and have healing lines almost weekly claiming people were healed through their ministry and then take credit for those healings. Some of those ministers have afflictions themselves and are not healed. I know of one minister that convinced people to bring their eye glasses to the Alter and stomp on them because God told him their eyes would be healed, they weren't. He didn't need glasses at that time, but had to get them along with all the others who stomped on theirs. He would probably blame the people's faith for not being healed. What about his faith? The problem I have here is he said God told him they would be healed. Was that a lie? I could share many stories when a minister said God told him people were healed, but they weren't. There are other ministers doing the same thing today and people still fall for what I call mans emotions. I believe in healing, but I believe it comes directly from God without the hype and mans emotions that you see in most healing lines. It becomes a show with people performing like you would see in a movie. The people that put on these shows walk away with bundles of the people's money for their performance. Some ministers are in it just for the money (false prophets).

My interest in what I'm saying is to make sure Christians are being told the truth. It is very important that the church hears the truth about His word and not an interpretation by some who believe they are the only ones that God speaks too. Being taught different interpretations of His word as is happening today causes the church to become very political. The church has become so political in our society today it is getting close to becoming another political party of our Federal Government. I believe that Reverend Billy Graham was close to becoming a candidate for President. When reading his autobiography he sure got close to some Presidents and appeared like he was included in some decision making. I believe God showed Rev. Graham what was happening and he returned to what God called him for. Billy Graham is my hero when it comes to preaching salvation. That's what it's all about, mans soul, not mans politics.

My observation of today's church is there is more political reason for attending than spiritual. If Ministers were honest they would have to say the function of the church operation is without a doubt riddled with politics. These same politics spill over into the spiritual realm causing disorder and improper function of the Body of Christ. God is showing me the Pastors roll in many cases has become a routine job in a secular society. When God calls people to fill the office of pastor, He means just that. Some of the responsibilities of a pastor are being a servant, overseer, and shepherd of the people, not a dictator or politician. Some people have filled this position for job security for themselves and their family. This sometimes gets into nepotism, not Gods calling.

God appoints whom He pleases, not man. No man calls you into a ministry office. It is a divine and supernatural call. I believe Paul's calling was supernatural. God alone calls men and women into ministry gift offices. If man is choosing who is next in line to teach or minister to the flock, it is wrong and we better take another look at what God's says. The Lord Jesus Christ Himself gave ministry gifts to the Body of Christ (Eph. 4:11). When Jesus said study to show thy selves approved, He didn't mean just Pastors, evangelist, prophets and teachers only, He meant everyone. If everyone would study the word and start asking questions, the leadership would have to start paying more attention to what they are teaching. This would start everyone down the right path to becoming one in Christ.

Over the years I've listened to ministers and teachers explain God's word and their personal or denominational interpretation of His word. They share how other Protestant and non-Protestant churches believe, agreeing or disagreeing with their interpretations. They would like everyone to think their interpretation is correct. I suppose this is why there are so many different denominations with their own interpretation of God's word. Does this mean that God speaks to one group and not the other or is one group more intelligent in interpreting the scriptures than the other? No, it means they agree with the interpretation they were taught without reading or studying His word. If more of the pew setters (laypeople) would read and study His word and speak up, maybe there wouldn't be so many different churches.

We are not living in Old Testament times. God speaks to all Christians, not just some. The Body of Christ needs to join together and stop disagreeing with each other and become one in Christ, then, it would function as God's word says it should. Remember, the prophet is subject to the prophets. Why don't the churches get together and have open discussions on all their different interpretations? It is because we can not humble ourselves and admit this is absolute nonsense to be acting like we do as the Body of Christ. If we expect the Body of Christ to function properly and be ready for HIS return, we better get our act together.

There is one portion of God's word most Christians do agree on and that is salvation. The remaining scriptures are up for grabs on how it might fit each denominational belief. If you follow some Ministers interpretation of God's word, they have concluded from their own intellect that some things in the Bible cannot be used for today's Christian. They say your self- esteem is more important than your conscience. They are trying to remove your conscience and do away with the Holy Spirit's conviction. If it makes you feel bad, don't worry, because it's not your fault, because God doesn't really mean what He says. It's not for Christians today. Some ministers are slowly eliminating certain scriptures to fit their agenda. In the future some Christian ministers will try to change what happened in the Garden. They will change it to say, Adam and Eve did no wrong so this should help peoples self-esteem. If Jesus doesn't return soon, the Bible will become extinct because some Christians will agree it is not for today. No one outside of the church will have to ban the Bible, the Government and intellectual Christians inside the church will slowly figure out how do away with it.

I believe in today's Christian church even though some are attending strictly to meet as a social gathering rather than to meet God with worship and praise as the body of

Christ. Some church services are dead in spirit (full of social politics), others are more in the flesh and they think they have God's power. After attending a church and listening to the canned sermons, controlled song and worship service, I am convinced that man controls everything without the Holy Spirit. The service starts at 11am and stops at 12-12:15pm. There are many other things happening in the church that I believe aren't scriptural and this is one of the reason why I have a problem participating. In the last church I was a member of the worship service was more like a sports outing, cheerleaders and all. We had coffee and donuts instead of hotdogs. The music was so loud I thought we had a University band playing. I couldn't hear myself sing or anyone else and some of the songs were new to me so I had a difficult time learning the melody. Worship and praise services should be lead by the Holy Spirit guiding the people. The gifts should be used for the edification of the body of Christ. Music instruments and songs of praise to God by the people should be encouraged and done in a way the Christian body can hear and understand. This is all done for the glory of God and the edification of the body of Christ. We need to remember we are not attending a sports or secular concert outing. The Holy Spirit is a gentleman and wants Christians to act the same and to represent the Father in a way that is respectful.

We have scheduled God in and out because that's the way we humans want it. We schedule the alter calls and stop when it looks like its time to stop. This reminds me of some that profess to have healing ministries. Everything is scheduled and only certain people are chosen for the healing line. The ones that are usually chosen are not the critical. We control everything and tell God when to show up. I know two ministers holding the office of pastor for many years and claim they were called by God, traveled the country hunting for so called prophets to give them a personal prophecy. They wanted a prophet to tell them how they were doing in their ministry and God's direction for the church. I don't understand why ministers of God have to do this, waste their time and money when all they have to do is ask God. He is with us at all times and is willing to communicate with us. He calls us and will guide us, not man. God will sometimes tell another person what you already know and this becomes a conformation to you. This will happen within your own ministry and you will not have to drive around the country looking for a prophet to tell you.

I believe there is a lack of balance and order of God's word in most churches. Some churches today operate in man's realm, not God's. Some ministers operate with their intellect, using control to operate the Body of Christ. The church (meaning the body of Christ) needs to get its' act together, repent, and pray God will have mercy on us all. Some churches claim revival is here but they have a difficult time recognizing the difference between mans emotions and the Holy Spirit. I believe one of the misconceptions about Christians today starting with ministers and teachers is they understand most of what they teach, but lack taking it serious. Laypeople see this and follow suit. This damages the body of Christ when not taking God's word serious. Most churches believe they are right in their doctrine so they have closed minds to any suggestions that might indicate they might be wrong. The sad part is the Christian world suffers because the church (body of Christ) cannot function properly, in balance. When reading about the Unity of Believers as Members of Christ body in 1Cor.12 (KJV), I don't understand why the Christian churches believe they can function properly. If the Body of Christ (Christians) can't put away their differences and come together, how do they ever expect to become one in Christ? We cannot become one in Christ by believing different doctrines. I can't find anything in God's word where it says God wanted man to develop all these different doctrines or that He would communicate with different people through vision or dreams about changing anything in His word.

I've observed some ministers and teachers that have good intentions when teaching, but I believe they are teaching things that are in direct contradiction to God's word. By doing this without recognizing the harm they cause to some in the body of Christ, they will develop unbalanced Christians and hypocrites without knowing it. New Christians will start their walk in an unbalanced way. If this type of teaching continues unchecked, it will continue to damage the Christian testimony to the world. All ministers and teachers need to pray that what comes from their mouths is from God, not man.

What has happened to the anointing of the Holy Spirit? From what I've observed in some churches, they are still looking for the Holy Spirit to come. We should not be asking the Holy Spirit to come when He is already here. If you're a Christian you already have Him within you. His activation in our lives is entirely up to us. I believe man has come to a point in his spiritual life where he has lost interest in seeking God for guidance and wants to try it on his own by using his intellect. This is very evident in today's message from some ministers. I see nothing supernaturally happening in today's Christian church. I'll remind you of the political aspects of what I said earlier, politics in churches today is becoming its' ruination. If the people will pray and ask God to allow the Holy Spirit to do His work and everyone allow this, things will change. God will speak to the hearts of people and then you will see real revival and not a revival of just man's emotions. It will be a true revival brought about by the Holy Spirit who is in control, not man. How can revival begin if man is in control? How will the church know when this happens? This will be new to everyone. God is not the God of confusion but a God of love and understanding and everything will be evident to all.

I'm afraid over this same period of time our churches have gotten into the same situation. The church has become a place of greed, controlled by politicians, and people are put into offices in the secular political way, not God's way. Money has become the main denominator, not faith. They have lost the people and especially the youth and now make all kinds of excuses why. TV ministries have taken advantage with the mega churches by asking for support from people who would usually support their home church. Of course they will not admit this, but it's the truth. I would like to sit down with these people and share with them how they are hurting the local churches. They are like the government politicians, not wanting to appear with anyone that might ask hard questions, because it might hurt their image. They are robbing the people just like the politicians are, filling their pockets with as much money as they can before they get caught.

If you don't believe this you're not keeping up with what is going on in our Christian society today. I could share with you many stories and facts about how ministers have taken advantage of the people over the years. Watching what is happening in our churches and on TV makes me sick to my stomach. The sad part of this is ministers are not standing up and defending God's word. They are doing as secular politicians do, looking out for themselves. Ministers and politicians are afraid if they upset anyone they might lose their position (job).

CHAPTER SIX

TEST THE PROPHETS

I BELIEVE IT'S TIME TO TEST THE PROPHETS

God gave us a way to test the prophets as was done in Jesus' time. We have that same authority today according to His word, but some ministers will not let that happen. Why? Because there probably is something wrong in Denmark as the saying goes. There could be sin within the church leadership. You know what I mean, secrets or wrong doings. I believe there are too many false teachers (ministers) in the Christian church today. God has showed me through the gift of discernment who some of these people are. If I named them you would only say I'm crazy. Please ask God to allow you the use of this gift and see what God shows you.

Some Ministers and Christian leaders should re-evaluate their calling. We might be surprised if the truth was told about how many false ministers there are in our Christian churches. Jesus said send the people out. Don't keep them in the church building for their entire life where it becomes nothing but a social gathering. This doesn't mean everyone has to quit their job or stop taking care of their family. It means Christians need to spend more time sharing the Gospel with other people besides the ones they see each week in their own church. The only way to do this is to train people. What would happen if people started leaving your church to minister and testify about God around the world? God would be pleased and the Holy Spirit would start replacing them with others and this would continue. Don't underestimate God and His supernatural powers. We have become to comfortable attending a social gathering each week and allowing the few to do our job. If you want to grow your church, teach people how to be fishers of men. Don't look for mans gimmicks to draw people in. Put your interest back where it should be, saving mans souls. People will come when they see how serious the minister and people are about spreading the Gospel. Develop programs together, take your disciples to homes and let them give their testimony about what God is doing in their lives. Just remember, this is for saving souls, not growing your church attendance and making money (greed). It is for growing God's church in Heaven.

If ministers are not satisfied with God's will in their lives and what they were called for, my advice is find a new career. Some ministers today are putting to much emphasis on numbers (mega churches, and money). They get upset if their membership and tithes don't increase to where they think it should be. It's all about mans ego. Whether new converts go to your church or not makes no difference, it's about saving souls. God will take care of the finances. God will supply all your needs (not what you think your needs are) if you're serious about doing what he commands you to do. Are we trying to please God or man? God is the Creator of all things, not man

There are some difference between the church today and when it was established in the New Testament. At the day of Pentecost the people worshiped God night and day. This means people were worshiping God in the churches day and night. This does not mean we have to be at the Wailing Wall 24/7. It means we should have God in our thoughts at all times, fellowshipping with Him. I'm sure if everything that happened during that period of time was put in the Bible it would show that the disciples had a life of their own. We can live a Christian life and enjoy things in life as long as we take God with us. There is a misconception about Christians not having a good time like people in the secular society. The Pentecostal churches that I've attended over the years have taken many scriptures out of context when it comes to dress, food, drink, social life, friends, movies, dance, etc. Pastors and youth leaders have a lot to do with church growth by the way they intermingle with the people. They must find the interest of the people and share that interest. People look up to spiritual leaders and they also want them to share fun time, especially the youth. As a leader you can't be a hermit or you will lose the people or your position in your church. God didn't put us on this earth to act like zombies.

The disciples taught the truth and didn't leave anything out. Some ministers today are afraid to teach the truth.

Why? They are afraid people will leave their church and there goes attendance and the money. I remember when ministers depended on God to provide for them and never failed to do so. Where has the trust in God gone? I believe in God's gifts. They are for the edifying and building up of the Body of Christ. Today these same gifts are being used by some to edify themselves, building their self-esteem and their egos. The gifts are being used for personal gains and most of the time they are taken out of context. I call it ego edifying.

For many years the Catholic and Protestant Church in this country have tried their best to destroy Christianity. Christians will blame all their problems on the secular society and they are partially right. Christians have slowly fallen for the same thing our first parents fell for, deception by satan. They are still doing this by slowly watering down the gospel and not telling the whole truth. It is not only the people within the church, but also people from the outside that are doing their best to corrupt and destroy the Christian Church. The corruption within both churches over the years has become one of the main problems why most people don't attend. I believe this is all caused by ministers not telling the whole story. If most Christians were serious about believing what God's word says and made use of the gifts guided by His Holy Spirit, all of this corruption would not happen. The problem is, in our churches today man does the guiding, not the Holy Spirit, and because of this the intellectuals and politicians are in control. These people believe they know what is best for everyone. The real problem is, most people believe them and fall for what ever they say. Christians should pray to God for real guidance and then stand up for the truth.

Another enemy of Christianity comes from other religions in this country. When the President of the United States says this is no longer a Christian country, he is saying soon we will no longer allow missionaries to spread the gospel. He is leading us straight to a one world religion. This sounds like we are returning to the time of the inquisitions during the Roman rule. Because this country believes in the freedom of religion we allow people from around the world of other religious beliefs to come in and build their worship centers and do their best to try and destroy Christianity. If these people say this is not true, ask them to go back to their countries and convince their leaders to allow Christians to do the same thing they are allowed in the U.S.A. They wouldn't dare. There have been many Christian missionaries around the world that have been killed or are in prison because of testifying about their God. How many people of different religious beliefs does this country have in prison for simply sharing about their god? None!!! You can buy their religious books in most book stores in this country. How many Christian books including the Bible can you find in countries with the Islamic faith? None!!!

CHAPTER SEVEN

QUESTIONS AND CONCERNS

WHAT HAPPENS WHEN YOU ASK QUESTION ABOUT THINGS HAPPENING IN THE CHURCH THAT CONCERN YOU? DO YOU GET AN AMSWER OR ARE YOU IGNORED?

God is showing me through His Holy Spirit that some leaders in the church are failing to tell the truth. I've noticed in church today, if you start asking questions or share concerns about the church, the pastor starts getting nervous, and some become paranoid. Just the thought that God is showing you something in His word and didn't show them first, blows their mind, especially if people start looking to you for answers. Their next step is to get rid of you before you start steeling their congregation. This has happened to me a couple of times in different churches I attended. I was only sharing with them what God was showing me. They forget they were called by God to their particular ministry, and if He wants them replaced, He will do it, not man. Where is their faith and trust in God? They accepted God's calling through faith, but when it comes to God protecting them, they lose their faith and trust in Him. Don't lose the vision God gives you and please don't change it to fit another vision (mans) which happens quite often.

The following is a true story about asking questions of concerns I had on certain things happening that didn't match God's word in a church my family and I were attending. The minister always said if you have any questions or concerns feel free to come to him and discuss them. In other words his office door was always open. This all sounded good until I started asking questions. We attended this church for about four years and I have yet to have a question answered. It sure sounded like politicians were in control and they didn't like my questions. They ignored me hoping I would go away, and eventually I did because my family and I were being attacked by gossip from so called Christians. Things got to a point where some would not speak to me and my family because of the lies that were being spread by a person with a Jezebel spirit. I knew there was a spirit of fear in some of the leadership. They brought this spirit of fear with them from another church they attended for many years. It eventually caused a split in that church and both churches have suffered ever sense. The church division was caused by fear and politics. Between the two, satan won the battle.

Before I explain all the circumstances that caused us to leave, let me explain briefly why we were going to this church. I was retired, enjoying life in my late fifties, but something was missing. God was impressing on me to teach and write about his word. I approached the Pastor and he said they were always looking for people to teach. After discussing this with the pastor and his wife things looked very positive. I believed this was an opening for me brought about by God, so I moved forward. My family and I started attending this church. We had attended this church a few years prior to this time so we were familiar with most of the people. I made it clear to the pastor that my wife and I were not looking for any positions (office) in the church. I was only looking forward to teaching.

I started working on a college degree in Bible theology which would eventually help me in teaching. I earned an Associates degree and completed about 80% of necessary studies towards a BS Degree. During all classes students were told by each instructor to ask question anytime they wanted to. This worked very well until I started asking questions that one instructor didn't like, so I was told I couldn't ask anymore questions. Because I reminded the instructor about the freedom to ask any and all questions I was asked not attend anymore. In other words they dismissed me. More about this college subject later. I started to see some things that just didn't match God's word, both in the college instruction and in the church teaching. I could also see some strife between some people and the leadership, so I started asking more questions. I soon found out there were three individual groups in the church. One group was only interested in hearing God's word. The second group was the politicians who only wanted to be close to the pastor and his wife (the inner circle). The third group was people wanting to share leadership roles or take over the ministry. This was not new to me because every church I ever attended had the same three groups. I tried to talk with some in each group to help solve the problems, it didn't work.

If I was seen outside of the church building talking to these people by the pastor or his wife I was accused of being a parking lot minister. I even suggested to the pastor setting down with everyone and have an open discussion and the answer was no (fear). The minister and wife never asked what was being discussed in the parking lot. I believe paranoia set in and assumptions were made and you know what "assume" means when you break it down. This is when things started to get ugly and the leadership clamed up. There were other things that happened and I won't mention them now that caused me to be very concerned. My questions were not being answered so I wrote a letter to the pastor hoping he would respond to it.

LETTER

Pastor, I am being accused of trying to divide the church, criticizing, and judging. God spoke to my heart to return to this church after some years of being absent. In the past three years I have tried to bring the message God gave me concerning things being out of order in the house of God. God also showed me through a vision to continue reading His word and He would show me the truth. He has given me many confirmations on what He has asked of me many times. Because of my aggressiveness and wanting to make sure the truth is being taught, some might think I am trying to take over your church. I assure you, that is the furthest thought in my mind. Has this task God gave me been easy for me? It certainly has not been. Has it been my choice?

It definitely was not. But in my obedience to God, I knew He would carry me through, if He ordained it, and He has. I spent forty years doing what I believe God wanted me to do and am very satisfied with how God helped me along the way.

I have no desire to lead a church at my age unless God would give me the vision, call me, which He has not done at this point in my life. My assignment has been to do only what God has commissioned me to do, and only that. I do believe God has given me a ministry for the church. I believe He anointed me years ago with oil just for this day. He anointed me, not man. Holy oil ran down my body and I felt the Holy Spirit doing His work. I have asked God why so long and He reminded me, it is in His time, not mine. When reading about the ministry in general, I believe you do not enter any phase just because you want to or because someone told you to and not even because someone prophesied to you. We forget what Jesus did for us and by doing what he did allowed us to communicate directly with the Father and not through a so called prophet. I would rather be guided by God than by man. I also believe no man calls you to the ministry, only God does this. He will position people whom He wishes into ministry gift offices. In the Old Testament education played an important part in the ministry. Samuel even instituted schools for prophets. This was done because God communicated through the prophets in the Old Testament, not necessary in the New Testament.

I have said in some of my letters that I am primarily interested in the body of Christ, making sure what is being preached and taught is the truth. God used many people in the New Testament to do just that and I believe He still does. Paul said, "Let the prophets speak two or three, and let the others judge" (I Cor.14:29 KJV). If the prophet's ministry is to be judged, then all other ministries would also need to be judged. You don't judge the person, you judge what they are preaching or teaching. You judge the person's ministry. This is not picking apart a pastor's sermons for any reason other than making sure it matches God's word.

After hearing responses about my letters to you from some in the congregation, it indicates fingers are being pointed at me, judging me without any opportunity to respond. I never understood how the people found out about my letters to you when you never responded to me. Could it be the Jezebel spirit? I am not responsible for the drop in attendance or the drop in tithing as some have accused me. Would you agree that the only way to resolve any differences is to sit down and discuss them using God's love? I have been open and honest about everything I've said to the entire congregation and have no guilt because God has asked this of me. I know if the church would follow this guideline and be open with everything, your church would move forward with the leading of the Holy Spirit. There should always be an open door, just knock and the door will open, Jesus kept no secrets. Being silent and talking about someone behind their back is not a way to solve any problem within the body of Christ.

The gossiping behind my back has caused some Christians in our church to fall into sin by succumbing to the carnal man and treating my family and myself coldly and definitely without God's love. Instead, they should have reacted as others have in our church showing God's love for all, even if they may not agree. They are truly the sons of God who can show God's love to all, regardless. This reaction by some tells me that God has work to do in your church both with leadership and with some in the congregation. Therefore, we need much teaching in this area. You see, there is teaching to be done. God truly walks with those who have not shunned us or treated us in a worldly way. But, woe to those who have not listened to God and continued to show His genuine love for the brethren because this does not please our Father. We belong to the same family.

In today's church, only God through His Holy Spirit will appoint whom He pleases and when He pleases into the ministry. They will be appointed to do certain works to make sure biblical truth and order is being taught to the body of Christ. From time to time God sends people that He appoints to a church with a message to stir believers up along a certain scriptural line. The person is sent just to do that. They are especially called of God with a distinct message to the church. They are not prophets. They carry words of wisdom to help solve out of order problems in the church. There are many who have been called to do this.

I offer this to help solve some misunderstandings. This letter indicates what I have been accused of dividing the church, so please consider the following:

1. Set up a meeting with the congregation to discuss my letters.

2. Ask why some think I'm trying to divide the church.

3. Ask why some think I'm pointing a finger, judging and criticizing.

4. Give me and the congregation an opportunity to voice our opinions.

If I am wrong, I will humble myself and apologize to all concerned. I will talk with and apologize if I caused them to leave and hopefully bring them back if I am in the wrong. If the leadership is in the wrong, I would expect the same from them. I am not trying to remove you or anyone else, only to do what God is requiring from everyone and that is doing things in order and teaching the truth.

END OF LETTER

This was one of many letters I wrote because I received no response from any leader in the church including the pastor. Then they wander why some Christians are not attending church. I am puzzled why Christian leadership is so afraid to defend their beliefs. Because the leadership in this church did not respond to my questions and concerns is an indication that I was right or they could not defend themselves by using God's word. Maybe some leaders live in fear that things might be uncovered that would put them on notice and maybe remove them from their position. Some leaders will lie, cover up their mess, or allow their Jezabel spirit to control things.

I know I am not the only one that sees and understands what is going wrong in the Christian church today. I have read many articles where God is showing others with the same concern and this becomes a confirmation to me. My observation is that everyone wants a piece of the action and the action is not God, it is power and money. Denominational leaders press their ministers for larger memberships and more or larger church buildings. Some ministers want to talk about mega churches and how much money they bring in. They are looking at greed, not souls for God. What happened to people being called by God and are more interested in mans souls then how big the church is or how much money is coming in. Christians need to start praying that these hypocrites (crooks) that are hiding behind sheep's wool will be cut off from the Body of Christ. The sheep's wool (disguise) sometimes comes in the person of Jezebel and is never exposed, especially in small churches. Christians need to pray for the real man of God to come, allowing the Holy Spirit to take control. The Holy Spirit knows what to do, and if we listen to Him, and follow His guide, everything will fall in line according to the will of the Father.

If we want to see great things happen, keep the Holy Spirit in control and the old man of sin out, especially the political man. All Christians should know what the scriptures say about the old and new man. In 2 Cor. 5:17(KJV) it says, "Therefore if any man be in Christ, he is a new creature: old things are passed away; and behold, all things are become new". The old man (sinner) was here before salvation and must leave after salvation. Many Christians want to keep the old man (sinner) in control because the new man (born again) wants change, and the old man doesn't. I would suggest by not changing and allowing the Holy Spirit to take control instead of satan, we are not very serious when we repent and accept Christ as our savior. Maybe the problem is because the Pastors or teachers didn't want to teach the truth about this scripture. Maybe they are keeping more of the old man than most people think. I have observed some ministers in the past and now that fit that category. I truly believe some ministers aspire to the pastor's position and are not called by God. There are many other reasons why some ministers are afraid. Examples: Fear (maybe I will have to follow the same teaching), or paranoia (maybe I will cause people to leave the church and this will mean the loss of tithes. Another example would be, (I might lose my position because people don't want to here the truth), or ego, (this might hurt my self esteem and I will lose favor with the people etc). The whole Christian system has become secular political.

The Christian leadership and we the people have failed God by not obeying His commands. We play church each week by putting more emphasis on the church budget, church politics, greed, bowing to people egos, and probably set under false doctrine because we don't listen and test the prophet (Pastors/Ministers). Jesus commanded us to become disciples and spread the word, not get comfortable in a building once or twice each week. There are some that worship the building and not GOD. Churches were supposed to be sanctuaries (Temples) for people to meet, worship, fellowship, and educate each other to go out and share the Gospel. Jesus did this and then taught his disciples, sending them out amongst the people. Any Pastor of a church has the responsibility to teach everyone about the word and set the example. This is done by what the world calls "on the job training". You train people and show them how to do it by taking them with you to demonstrate how it's done. You don't just tell them and expect them to go do it. Our church buildings should be schools for educating and training all Christians for sharing the Gospel of Jesus Christ wherever they travel. All Christian leadership and laypeople need to understand there are four distinctive personalities. For some it's easy to speak out and for others it's very difficult. This is another failure of Christian leadership, not seeing the problem and addressing it. Everyone is not a red (out spoken) personality.

To close this chapter did you ever notice that during the past fifty to seventy years the Catholic and some Protestant churches have had the most problems with their Ministers and Priest? It has been a combination of different types that over time have done their damage and it has had a very negative effect on membership and new converts. These types are still at work within the Christian church. If the Pentecostal churches believe what they say about the Baptism in the Holy Spirit giving them power to discern bad spirits, why isn't it happening? This is why I believe Christians in general play church. I would be glad to sit down with any Pentecostal and discuss why I believe they play church and back it up with scripture. I've always felt that most Catholics needed to read their Bible and educate themselves. From what I've observed most Catholics follow what ever comes from the Vatican without even asking whether it's Biblical or not. I am starting to believe the same thing about the Protestants. I believe most of them follow mans interpretation instead of asking the Holy Spirit to guide them in the truth.

CHAPTER EIGHT

A Brief Christian History

Where I attended church the Christians leaders had no interest in learning or teaching about other religions. I tried to convince them because I believe Christians need to know all about them, where they started, why they are so different from Christianity. I strongly recommend all Christians read and learn about how these other religions were formed and compare them to Christianity. I ask a Christian minister one time why these religions were not discussed and the response I received was they were afraid they might lose the people to the other religion. Is this kind of thinking, trusting in God? I've always believed if you have an opponent trying to prove you wrong in anything, especially your Christian beliefs, you need to know as much as possible about them to help you defend Christianity. Read God's word about knowing your enemy.

I would like to share with you how the Romans forced their Christianity on the world when they were in power.

This could be an example of what is to come with another religion if we don't start fighting back. If you want to know about the future, you better start reading the Bible, it's all true, and no one can prove it different. Some people in our Government would probably want the Bible to become extinct or have it re-written to meet the requirements of a world religion. I believe some Christian ministers have already started in that direction.

In the following paragraphs I want to share what I know about some history of the Catholic Church and how it did some bad things in their development over the years. It is only to show how man makes mistakes because I believe they leave God out of their decision making. I am not just picking on the Catholic Church to put it down. The Protestant Church has done things in the past that also need some attention. I believe both churches have over the years caused the problems we see today and why people don't want to attend.

After the original twelve Apostles the Romans declared Christianity their official religion. This made a way for the Catholic Church to develop their doctrines. This also made the church quite different from what Jesus taught. One of the problems I always had a difficult time understanding was, Jesus told us to "call no man your father upon this earth", for one is your father in heaven. They give the title of Father to its' Priest. What should we do with what the word clearly says "all have sinned", but the Catholic Church says the Pope is perfect and infallible? I believe the Catholic Church has always said their congregation should not study the Bible. They are to leave it up to the Pope and his clergy to interpret God's word. This is a contradiction because the word says every man should "read it all the days of his life". Catholic leadership has always opposed common man reading the scriptures for themselves. What are they afraid of? I believe they are afraid the people will come to a conclusion that the Catholic leadership has misinterpreted the scriptures. There are some Catholics that have done exactly that and some have converted to Protestantism. This has happened many times over the past forty years.

Going back in time the Catholic Church would give severe penalties to those that were caught reading the Bible, even death. This also would happen when it came to punishment for opposing church doctrine during the Inquisition. So if you were a non-conformer you were a heretic, someone who is opposed to a church doctrine. Can you imagine this happening today? If I was a Catholic I would be a heretic because I not only disagree with some of their doctrine, but also some doctrine of the Protestant religion. They would put me in prison and throw away the key. You were a heretic if you did not believe our Lord the Pope had power. The Bible calls this blasphemy.

When reading world history I was amazed at how the Catholics treated Protestants during the Inquisition which included whippings, tortured, galleys, and death for challenging the Pope. There was a Spanish Catholic by the name of Juliano and sometime during the 16th century he visited Germany and was exposed to the Bible. What he read caused him to abandon the Catholic religion. He started smuggling Bibles back into Spain and was caught, arrested, along with people that were accepting the Bibles.

They suffered the consequence and were tortured, burnt, roasted upon spits, imprisoned for life, publicly whipped and some sent to the galleys.

One of the prophecies given by Jesus was, "an hour is coming when whoever kills you thinks and claims he has offered service to God". This should sound familiar to everyone because what is said about the Islam religion today. Read the Koran. The Roman Catholic Priest was the Inquisitors working for the church. God's word talks about false teachers, "who come disguised as harmless sheep, but are wolves. There has been and still are people around the world who claim to be God or Jesus and even the anti-Christ. Even Popes in history have claimed to be God. I believe Pope Nicholas was one and Constantine believed it. The Catholics taught by paying money to the church, they could release the souls of dead people who were confined in the tormenting flames. This was called "Indulgence". The Pope allowed this as another chance to buy your way out of hell. Where in God's word did they get this from? This sound like another of mans way of saying I am in control. Here is another one of mans false prophecies, the 264th Pope will be the last man to hold the office. Pope John Paul II was the 264TH Pope. This was a Catholic prediction and it did not occur because it is mans prediction. It came from the flesh and not the spirit.

In the twelfth century the Catholic Church was having problems getting new converts. So they started following the practices of their religious competitors. There primary rivals of the early Catholic religion were Iris of Egypt, Ishtar of Babylon, and Athena in Greece. These religious sects were followers of the Pagan Goddess. This is when the Catholic Church began to emphasize the role of the Virgin Mary hoping this would broaden the appeal to their religion. This was in desperation by the Roman Church at that time to compete for new converts. This is similar to what is happening today in some of the churches. They are competing by using mans gimmicks to compete for new converts. Coffee, donuts, pastries and many dinners have become the competition between churches to draw people. It's not bad enough that a high percentage of people in this country are obese and now the church is contributing to this by feeding their congregation fat food. They are using food as their idol.

The Bible teaches that there is only one mediator between God and man and that is Jesus. The Catholic Church continued through the twelfth and thirteenth centuries to promote the doctrine of Mary as the "co-redeemer with Christ. I believe they knew this was not true, but out of desperation to not lose in the competition for converts they continued and still do today. This can not be found in God's word. They only did this to compete with other religions for converts. The church has stated that Mary was free of sin. She become equal to Jesus in status and people quickly believed in the power of Mary. In some parts of the world Catholics still worshiped her in place of Christ.

The following are some reasons why I believe our Government and other Governments would like to see a "one world religion". They believe this would cause everyone to live in peace. The problem is we don't all believe in the same God. Some do agree there will be an end time as do scientist. Scientist believes there was a beginning and there will be an end. Scientist might not agree with Christians and other religious groups on how it will happen, but they still believe it will take place.

EXAMPLES: HOW SOME RELIGIONS EXPLAIN HOW THIS WORLD WILL END.

1. Christians (people who believe there is one God and His son is Jesus Christ) believe in the Old and New Testaments, also believe there will be a time of stress and (tribulation). This is called the end times.

2. Muslims believe in the Islam religion and the Koran says, before the Kingdom of Allah can be fulfilled "a time only known to God", a horrible calamity will occur when the earth will be shaken. Then the trumpet will be sounded. The Korans description of tribulation is similar to the Christian Bible.

3. The Jewish faith refers to this as a distress that is great, so that none is like it: it is even the time of Jacob's trouble (end times).

4. Hindu sects say there is one man named Swami Bhaktipada, is currently preparing "twelve walled cities that he believes will be the salvation of the human race. The twelve cities will accommodate twelve thousand people each, which equal 144,000 (end times).

5. There are some Old Catholic prophecies that project similar destruction.

6. Regarding Babylon, Jeremiah wrote "a nation from the north will attack her and lay waste her land. Another verse describes Iraq's destroyer as a "Great Nation. Could it be Russia or China? They are all in the North. The real question, who will be the real Babylon? Some believe the United States is the destroyer from the North. I believe everything that is going to happen will come from the area around the Middle East. That is where God started everything and this is where he will end it.

Note: man has made many predictions, some have happened, and some not. We need to stop listening to man and read and study God's word, because it is the truth.

Closing this chapter out is very difficult for me. I would like to continue to write about the church and its problems but I need to continue on with the rest of the book. I would like to say this, if you want to know what has happened to the church, take a good look at how things have changed in our society throughout history. It is important that we understand where the church was and where it is going as far as continuing the work that God wants done. The church is slowly dying because of the lack of truth and unity. Unity within the church means all Christian believers not just one denomination. The church is the body of Christ, the whole body, not just an arm and a leg. Man needs to humble himself and ask God for forgiveness, stand up and represent the Father like they should using the power given them by His Son Jesus Christ. Many Christians today are still attaching themselves to the same idols our ancestors attached themselves to. It's all about the intellect. We believe more in ourselves than we do in God. The problem is separating our flesh from our spirit and that is difficult. We need to try harder!

This is my opinion of religions and their beliefs in this country. Because of these different beliefs Christians should take a real good look at how man over the years has taken control with their thinking and understanding of what God is saying in His word. The intellectual man thinks he knows more than God. It's amazing how man can take God's Book and interpret it so many different ways. I believe it comes down to what ever fits their agenda and how they want to live their lives is how they interpret His word.

CHAPTER NINE

CHANGE

Has God's word about winning souls for Christ changed? Has the church stopped teaching Christians how to evangelize? Is changing how a Church Sanctuary looks or how the worship service is conducted, God's way of winning souls? Has coffee and donuts and dinners taken the place of what the Bible says a Christian really needs for nourishment? Is the secular world now controlling what the church needs to win souls? Do we Christians need to get back to the basics, reading His word daily, trusting God and His word, praying, follow in the footsteps of His Son Jesus, being obedient and increase our faith in Him?

The following is one of the reasons why my wife and I have a difficult time attending church in our Christian society today. The following happened in a denominational church in the near past. Before I explain how I believe some ministers and laypeople have lowered God's standards in His place of worship, let me share with you some thoughts about sanctuaries, tabernacles, and temples. Without going into all the details you can find in the Bible or Bible dictionary, which is where you will find very good definitions for all three, I will try to condense my thoughts about what they say.

The Hebrew definition for sanctuary is "to be clean" and/or "to be holy" and it appears 60 times in Exodus, Leviticus, and Numbers. I believe that means spiritually and physically clean. Sanctuary refers to a place where God appeared and/or dwelt, as indicated by the presence of the Ark. The patriarchs had places to worship, so when ever God was speaking to them, they would build an Alter and pitch their tent to sacrifice and worship God. Scriptures to read are found in (Gen.26:24, 25 and Heb.8:5, 6 KJV).

Tabernacle is another place the people used for worship. A tabernacle was called "Sacred residence", "sanctuary", or "holy place". Check any Bible dictionary for all of its uses and how sacred it was inside.

Temple is another form of sanctuary. David wanted to build a dwelling place for God, but in his lifetime because of wars, he never did. David accumulated the necessary finances, purchased the materials, and drew the blueprints, but his sons ended up building the temple (house for God). There were other temples built in the Old Testament, such as Solomon's, Zerubbabel's, Herod's and Ezekiel's. Check a Bible dictionary for their use.

All sanctuaries in the Old Testament were places to meet with God to worship Him, and sacrifice the blood of animals before God. Even Christ showed respect for the temple. He even threw the money changers out because it was God's temple. He described it as "the house of God' or his Father's house. After the day of Pentecost the early church used the temple (church) as a meeting place. It was surely not a place to play games. As I said, this is a condensed overview and if you need more understanding, read any good Bible dictionary on the subjects.

Because of what God's son did, giving His life for all mankind by dying on the cross to save us from our sins, he become the last sacrifice. No other sacrifice is necessary. On the day of Pentecost we became His Spiritual Temple. According to the New Testament we all should know where God's dwells. He dwells in the believer and his body is God's temple. This is why Paul used the term "Body of Christ". We Christians all belong to the body of Christ. But, we still need a meeting place to gather for fellowship with other Christians and worship God along with being taught about His word, so they built church buildings in Paul's time and this continued and still does today. I don't believe God wanted Christians to build a church building on every street corner because of our different views on what His word says. Study the New Testament and you might conclude that church buildings are not necessarily needed today, because we are the church. Jesus called twelve men to become fishers of men, taught them and sent them out to evangelize the world. I guess you could say the reason for having church buildings in the time of Paul and today is for people to separate themselves from the sinners and show unity while being taught. Somewhere along the way we have lost the unity by allowing man to take the place of the Holy Spirit.

Many church buildings (sanctuaries) were built over the years of different architectures and always seemed to end up being nothing but idols for people to hold onto and worship, instead of God. Christians can fellowship and worship God wherever and whenever they want. I believe this is where the trouble starts, because it's easier for satan and his army to join the church group and play his game of deception. Satan does this by coning people into playing politics and in most cases starts a division within the congregation and he loves this kind of war. It is more beneficial for him to use crowd deception then it is to deceive people one at a time. Believe me this is done by many false prophets (Pastors) that are only interested in themselves and their greed. If Christians could keep secular politics out and God's Spirit in, the church would flourish and be more effective around the world. When Christians start asking God's Spirit to get involved instead of church politicians the false prophets will not be able to steel or even be in office.

If the pastor is not a strong Spiritual leader he will lead people down the wrong path. In other words, if politics are leading, and not the Holy Spirit, it's the wrong path. Christians that are really serious should not be afraid to approach the pastor, and discuss his walk with God. He should be serious and up front with everyone. Some churches that are politically motivated eventually split because of all the different politics being played. The problem with this is, after the split occurs both sides continue to play politics. No one ever wants to set down

SAMUEL D. SCULL

and discuss why this is happening. Both sides think they're right and if discussed would end up finding out they were both wrong. Most church splits are human secular based and not spiritual based. What we need are honest people, called by God, who will stand firmly against these satan deceived people and teach them the truth. That means deny satan entrance into your body and the sanctuary built by Christians for fellowship and the worship of God. Politics in the church will cause strife and division. This allows the secular world to see how hypocritical some Christians are. The church building where Christians are supposed to meet to worship God has become like any other building used for secular reasons. There is a lack of respect for God's sanctuary (church building) in the Christian society today. It is sometime very hard to tell the difference between the Church buildings and some secular Town Halls with all the crooked politicians.

I'm not saying we shouldn't meet as part of the body of Christ, I'm saying we use the church building as an excuse to only worship God once/twice per week. All church buildings should be open seven days per week for worship, fellowship and the teaching of God's word and the more teaching the better. I believe if we were serious about living for God and we were following His commands, he would provide the finances to keep the doors open seven days a week. Trust in the Lord and He will supply all our needs. What Paul said in the following scriptures will happen without anyone knowing it. We would all be in a revival. God's power would be revealed to the world and great things would happen. We are so far from becoming a single body of Christ and the Church without spot or wrinkle, it is pathetic. The following is how Paul explained the Body of Christ.

1 Corinthians: 12: 12-27 (KJV)

12. For as the body is one, and hath many members of that one body, being many, are one body: so also in Christ.

(Example) Our human bodies have many members but are all included as one. For the church is one, and hath many members of that one body, being many: also in Christ.

13. For by one spirit are we all baptized into one body, whether we be Jews or Gentiles, whether we be bond or free; and have been all made to drink into one spirit.

(Example) For by God's Spirit we are all baptized into one body (church), whether we are Jews or Gentiles, free or bond, and we all drink of the same Spirit.

14. For the body is not one member, but many.

(Example) This is comparing the human body to the body of Christ (church). For the church is not one member, but many (all members in all churches believing in one God and His Son Jesus Christ as their Savior and the Holy Spirit as their comforter and guide.

15. If the foot shall say, because I am not the hand, I am not the body, it is therefore not of the body?

(Example) If any Christian shall say, because I am not the prophet, I am not part of the body, he is therefore not part of the body

16. And if the ear shall say, Because, I am not the eye, I am not of the body, is it therefore not of the body?

(Example) is the same as v15.

17. If the whole body were an eye, where were the hearing, where were the smelling?

(Example) If the people (body of Christ) were all Pastors, where were the teachers, where were the students?

18. But now hath God set the members, everyone of them in the body, as it has pleased Him.

(Example) But now hath God set all Christians (church) in the body (Jesus Christ), as it pleased Him. It is not our place to chose where we fit in the body of Christ, this belongs to Him.

19. And if they were all one member, where were the body?

(Example) And if they were all arms, where are the other body members that make up the body?

20. But now are they many members, yet but one body.

(Example) we are many members, and become one body functioning at God's will.

21. And the eye cannot say unto the hand I have no need of thee: nor again the head to the feet, I have no need of you.

(Example) And the pastor cannot say to the other members, I have no need for you: nor can any member say to another, I have no need for you. All the members have to function to make sure the body is in balance.

22. Nay, much more those members of the body, which seem to be more feeble, are necessary.

(Example) All members of the body of Christ are necessary regardless of there situation. God is not a respecter of persons.

23. And those members of the body, which we think to be less honorable, upon these we bestow more abundant honor; and our uncomely parts have more abundant comeliness.

(Example) God is not a respecter of persons. He treats us all on the same level and loves us all the same. You can't gain favor with God over another through your education, political position etc.

24. For our comely parts have no need: but God hath tempered the body together, having given more abundant honor to that part which lacked:

(Example) We are His creation and He loves us for accepting His son. He wants all Christians to be of one body, not separated by different doctrines. In His eye we are all at the same level.

25. That there should be no schism in the body; but that the members should have the same care one of another.

(Example) There should be no division or split in the Body of Christ (church), not differences of opinion, of doctrine etc. This includes the whole body of Christ (all Christian churches) not just the head, hand, or foot, the whole body. This means all Christian churches should get along with each other under the same doctrine.

26. And whether one member suffers, all the members suffer with it; or one member be honored, all the members rejoice with it.

(Example) this verse speaks for itself.

27. Now ye are the body of Christ, and members in particular.

(Example) If we follow these scriptures and do not deviate from them our Christian society would be where God wants us, all of one body, not thousands of bodies, all believing and going down different paths. We would be the light to the world. Today the light is getting very dim.

Note: I believe God is telling us the whole body of Christ should be in unity, and not just individual denominations. I believe the body of Christ is so out of balance, because of man being in control for so long, and he doesn't want to get out of the way and allow the Holy Spirit to do what He was sent for. Man took control along time ago in the Garden, and he is still having a tough time giving control back to

God. When we look at how far the church has gotten off Gods path and how long they've been there, it would seem impossible to gain unity. But, God does perform miracles, if we would just let His Holy Spirit take control, and guide us in the right direction.

Who is God? We humans with our finite minds, always underestimate who He is and what He can and will do if we follow His guidance. We make our decisions and justify what we do without God and then wonder why our Christian society is so splintered. Trust is where we humans fall short. God is looking for people who will trust and obey.

I attended two churches that only paid attention to certain people and not to others about their concerns. I was surprised when one minister had an open door policy for everyone who was interested in what was happening in the body of Christ. When we first started attending this church, I'll never forget what the pastor said, and I quote "there are no secrets here and we will not have any". This is what we wanted to hear and we hoped there would be no lies. We seen and heard things we felt were of God because they were scriptural and some things we felt were not scriptural. So we continued looking at things through our spiritual eyes, matching them with God's word, and His will. My wife and I had many discussions about our concerns with the pastor at his request. All Pastors should have an open door policy for discussions with everyone, not just a few.

We had respect for the pastor as we do for all pastors. Why? According to the word God chooses and anoints the ones He wants to lead His church. In this particular church only one shepherd was leading the flock and making decisions. At least that is how it looked on the surface. After being exposed to the leadership for a short period of time we found things to be different. There were more than two shepherds and this was causing confusion to the flock (congregation). Its bad enough having two, but three or more, having different personalities, and are not one in unity with each other and God, is bordering on the ridiculous.

The pastor asked for input to help the body of Christ, and said there would be no secrets. We believed what he was saying, so we shared with him and continued to do so. I shared with another pastor using oral and written input about certain things I observed that were out of order in the church, using scripture. He accepted my comments and we discussed them on many occasions. He agreed with my interpretation of the scripture but never took action to correct some situations that were out of order and not scripturally correct.

There were other things we discussed of a similar nature, being out of order, but he took no action to correct them. I believe this is where the politics started. I believe he shared my beliefs which he agreed with, with others and this caused the politics to enter. These corrections would have to take place with people in his inner circle, so corrections to things that were wrong and not scriptural never took place. The sad part of this was, the pastor never communicated back to me. Why? I never found out. He slowly stopped communicating with me. This is what happens in our Christian society today when internal church politics take place. The church politicians control some Pastors.

The real problem started when the minister and some laypeople started gutting the inside of a beautiful sanctuary because they believed the change would bring in more people, especially the youth. Increasing the membership was the pastor's assignment from headquarters and apparently they didn't care how it was done. This approach was completely different from how I had been taught about how people are brought into the body of Christ. It was taught to me that we are servants as Jesus was when here on earth. It is our responsibility to go out and bring them in, so this is what my wife and I were doing. God brought in approximately thirty new people to the church by using my wife and me. This is done by prayer and the Holy Spirits guidance. We are to share the Gospel (salvation) and let the Holy Spirit do the convicting. Once we have done our part God will take over. Mans problem is, he has lost trust in God doing His part. In the first place, who are we trying to please, God or man? The pastor was satisfied with the increase in membership. This is what he was charged with and he might get a promotion to a church where he could retire from.

My mistake was not using the gift God gave me the minute I walked through the church door and that is the gift of discernment. The minister used me and my wife to do what he couldn't do, and that was to bring people into the church through his preaching and teaching which in turn would increase the membership. This is what he was required to do and it looked good on his monthly report to Denominational Headquarters. According to him this was his last church to pastor because he was dismissed from six or seven other churches (his own words). It must have looked good to headquarters because they move him to another church as an assistant pastor which he told me he would never do.

I remember attending another church for about 25 years where trust in God came first. Most of the people were very dedicated Christians and appeared to be in unity with Christ and each other. This unity included everyone, the youth (unmarried), young married couples, older married couples and singles. Some shared the Gospel on the street corners, in homes, in other churches in four States etc. They had a lay-witness program that would reach out to as many churches as possible in New Jersey, Delaware, Pennsylvania, and Maryland. This was not to proselytize and increase the home church attendance. It was all about winning souls for Christ and helping other churches. This was building unity within the body of Christ. It was sharing our testimony with who ever would listen. Even back then God showed me through the gift of discernment a problem in the home church. Through the lay-witness program God showed me who was really trusting in Him and who were the typical political hypocrites in the home church.

There was a certain group of people who would always steer clear of the lay-witness weekends. These people would rather stay at the home church for weekend services and God showed me why. These people were jockeying for positions in the church and were afraid to go on a mission because someone else in the group might move ahead of them in a leadership roll. It was like watching a secular political bid at election time. All they had to do was pray and trust in

God, because he will use you where He wants you, not where you think or someone else thinks you should be. God knows you better than you do or someone else. This is what I mean when I say man has taken control, he wants to run the church and leave God out. Mans intellect and ego continues to control him.

We fail to share the Gospel and bring new people into the fold allowing the Holy Spirit to deal with their spirit. We then look for ways to bring them in by using mans gimmicks. Coffee and donuts have taken the place of Christians sharing their testimony with others. We get canned sermons and written guidelines on how the service is to be structured. It makes no difference whether the Holy Spirit is moving on the "body of Christ", because man says it all starts and stops at a certain time. Instead of taking time for personal testimonies, time is taken for coffee and donuts. Some churches have replaced Sunday school with play time for the kids. They can play table tennis, shoot pool, pinball and even watch TV. This particular church didn't want to teach children how to tithe by bringing in their coins just because they didn't like counting them. The pastor said if you couldn't put paper money in the collection, don't bother putting in anything.

By the way, remember what I said about no secrets, this was a secret. The youth didn't like the décor of the sanctuary so they wanted it changed to their liking and the pastor agreed. There are quite a few churches that are doing similar things for the sake of the youth. This is all okay if the youth are serious about God and what His Son Jesus did for us. Are they following the guidelines of the Holy Spirit and working towards winning souls for Jesus, or are they just wanting to be seen, you know what I mean, boosting their egos. There have been many changes over the past twenty to thirty years in the youth development in our society. I believe we have slowly raised our youth to a point where they believe they should have control of both societies, secular and Christian, and it has affected the church in a negative way. If they didn't get their way they surprised the congregation by removing all the pews and installed tables and chairs, table cloths, and candles. This was done without the congregation and members knowing it until Sunday morning service. (a secret)

CHAPTER TEN

HONOR YOUR PASTOR

If I understand God's word as a Christian should, we are to read, study, and make sure we are doing what God's word says. If we don't, we become like the world, which means we never accepted the change that took place the day we were born again. Remember at salvation we accept Jesus as our savior and ask forgiveness of our sins, and a new spiritual man is born, the old spiritual man dies. We Christians have a tough time stopping the old man from resurrecting himself. I know it's a battle, but we can win if we are serious about being a new creature in God. Jesus won His battle and we are to follow in His footsteps. If we sway to the right or left we will get in trouble. God was showing me things happening in the church that were not scriptural according to His word and it became a concern to me. I believe the church is either way left or way right and can't seem to find the middle (balance). Some Christians take certain scriptures as gospel and other scriptures they could care less about. I call it the pick and chose doctrine.

At the time of my concerns I was not trying to gain the favor of the pastor to gain a position in the church. I was not trying to remove him from office or take the church from him. I was just trying to point out what God was showing me about some serious problems in the church. The Pastor understood that I was serious and did listen to some of my concerns, but never offered to discuss them. So he and his wife started what I call a smoke screen (to hide, cover up, disguise etc.). That was the defense system they decided to use. They started telling the congregation that someone in the church was creating strife and it had to stop. Then a Jezebel spirit surfaced and the gossip started, so we as a family eventually left the church. After reading this article, I decided to tell the both sides of the story. But before I make my comments, I would like to remind everyone that I believe in God's word as being the truth. If you don't tell the whole truth about God's word you're wasting your time.

When it comes to leadership, education is not always the answer. I do believe in education and the more education you receive, if used properly, is a benefit to all. Some of my comments about education are to show that the best leaders are not always College/University educated people. Remember, and please don't take me wrong, I do believe in education. These five items will help everyone understand how the church has drifted in the wrong direction.

1. A call to the ministry: Jesus Christ is the only one who does this, not man. (Mk. 1:17, 20, 2:14, Lu. 6:13; Jn.1:43; Ac.22:21; Eph. 4:11 (KJV). I don't read in any of these scriptures where it says education

is a requirement for this office. God knows who He wants to lead and He is the educator. His way of educating people using His Holy Spirit is so much better then mans way of doing it.

2. I believe some pastors today have not been called by God. They are either appointed because they went to Bible College, they are part of the family in charge or politics are being played. This becomes job security for the family or friends. Some people with the gift of gab and some Bible knowledge aspire (not called) to this office for many reasons (I'll let you guess).

3. Some people who are Bible College educated are not necessarily qualified to hold any office mentioned in Eph. 4:11 simply because they were not called by God. It is not your intellect that God is interested in, it's your heart.

4. Some Christians that graduate from secular colleges and attend church think they deserve to be the leader, but unless called by God, they are wasting their time. This is not a game of politics, it is serious business having to do with man's salvation and being obedient to God.

5. When going down this road listed in (2, 3, 4) the church ends up a secular led church, leaving God's Holy Spirit out. Some leaders that are well educated start forgetting who is in control. All Christians should know that the Holy Spirit is in control, not man. Of course God recognizes He gave man a free

> will and man can do as he pleases so he continues
> to be in control.

I would like to share with you an article called "In Your Pastor's Honor" that was made available to everyone in the church I was attending. I believe this article was used by the leadership to defend the pastor because of my concerns about things happening in the church that God showed me to be wrong and out of order. At the end of this chapter I will explain how I believe the church has moved so close to doing things in a secular way rather than a Christian way and they don't even know it. This article was written on two sheets of 8X11 paper without any notice of rights reserved.

After reading this article, I have concluded that the writer of "In your Pastor's Honor" is like many others only telling one side of the story. Numbers 16, is a good reference when it comes to conspiracy and envy, especially if that is happening in your church. The first thing a pastor needs to do before referring to Num. 16 is to make sure this is happening. I can recall a pastor being afraid of the same thing, thinking there was a conspiracy to take his church, but all it was is fear, paranoia, and the thought of losing his control. I also believe there was deception occurring as well. Some churches allow the spirit of Jezebel to enter in allowing the spirit of fear, deception, paranoia, and control to take over. Also, there are some biblical scholars attending church who are more interested in playing politics than helping the pastor and the body of Christ. Some people are always trying to take over because they believe they can do it better because they are better educated and they deserve it.

This article reminds me of some of the rhetoric used by some pastors trying to put fear into people who might disagree with them. The spirit of fear and paranoia can be so strong in some leaders that they think they are losing control and it frightens them, causing strife, and some times division. Some people whether in the congregation or leadership always have a tough time admitting they're wrong. The writer needs to tell the whole story and not just try to make it look like it is always someone else's fault.

As it's been said many times from the pulpit, we are all human and make mistakes. I believe if we don't have a check and balance, it will always be one-sided. This could be detrimental to both pastor and congregation. The writer talks about Moses and Aaron and the opposition they faced with Karoh, Dathan and Abiran, and the earth opened up and consumed them. The other side of this story is, if Moses had not been listening to God, the earth might have opened and consumed him instead of the way it did happen. The rebellion might have been legal and God might have removed Moses and Aaron. Remember, Moses was not allowed into the Promised Land because of what, disobedience. This is the other side of the story.

The following is a list of responses that are numbered to correspond to the article. They are numbered also to help you compare my responses.

IN YOUR PASTOR'S HONOR

YOU MAY NEVER KNOW HOW DEEPLY YOUR PASTOR AND THE MEMBERS OF YOUR

PARSONAGE FAMILY APPRECIATE THE PRAYERS YOU OFFER ON THEIR BEHALF.

ARTICLE:

1. Numbers 16 tells an interesting story. Korah, Dathan and Abiram were not happy with the conditions of their community, and they went as a group to oppose Moses and Aaron, their shepherds. They questioned Moses as their appointed leader, and they ask Moses and Aaron. "Why then do you set yourselves above the Lord's assembly?" perhaps the three of them felt they were equally qualified to lead the Israelites to the promise land.

MY RESPONSE:

1. Numbers 16 is a very interesting story about how God protected His servants in the Old Testament. God only chose certain people in the Old Testament to represent Him to do what He commanded, and by being obedient, He protected them. He also chastised Moses by not allowing him into the Promise Land. God's balance, you make a choice, you answer for it. This is the other side of the story.

Remember, these were Old Testament prophets who had the spirit of God upon them, and all others were dead in spirit. In the New Testament all Christians on the day of Pentecost became spiritually alive and have the Holy Spirit in them. Only Moses and Aaron had guide lines from the Holy Spirit to help them. God speaks to all Christians in the New Testament, not just pastors. If you're called and anointed of God to stand in the office of Pastor, there are many scriptures that He commands you to adhere too. 1Tim. 3 is a good example and we are all subject to the same guidelines.

If a pastor is not abiding by these commands, we as Christians (members of the Body of Christ) have the right to be concerned, and the right to use Mt.18. Just as a reminder, if we have sin in our lives we should not be using Mt.18 because we become hypocrites. Hypocrisy is a sin. God's word is not just for pastors or their wives to use to help other Christians. If we go down that road some ministers could get away with murder. I believe one of the biggest problems in our Christian community today is hypocrisy, and the world sees it.

Most pastors will use this defense: Who do they think they are, pointing the finger at me, after all, I am the chosen one (like Moses) in this church, so I should not be questioned about anything. In church today, this is called a smoke screen. There is nothing in the N.T. that says you can't test the prophet. Besides, if the pastor is doing what is required of him according to God's word, why should he worry about being tested by other Christians? If he is right in what he is doing it will come out in a discussion using God's word to settle it. Besides, if Christians (spiritually alive) who talk to God as the pastor can, he should be concerned also and want to know what he or she might be doing wrong.

ARTICLE:

2. They questioned Moses as their appointed leader.

MY RESPONSE:

2. In New Testament teaching, I see no scriptures against asking questions to check the authenticity of what is happening in the church. If we go down the road that Christians with the Spirit of God in them cannot ask questions of concern, we are saying Gods word is not true. Remember the gifts are available to all Christians, not just pastors or their wives. If they were only available to a few we would still be living in Old Testament times. I would remind you of all the false teachers who have surfaced in the past twenty to forty years, especially in the United States. Everyone should be free to ask all the questions they need answered as long as there is no conspiracy or envy on their part. A true man of God in a pastor's position, knowing he was called of God, should not operate in fear or paranoia.

ARTICLE:

3. When Moses heard their opposition, he proposed a "trial of fire," telling them, "In the morning, the Lord will show who belongs to Him and who is holy." When the assembly gathered in the morning, God opened up the earth and swallowed Korah, Dathan and Abiram and all their possessions and households- hymnals and all. They were destroyed because they spoke out against their pastor.

MY RESPONSE:

3. I do believe if there is a conspiracy, people wanting to overthrow the leadership appointed by God, He will still deal with them. I also believe if the shoe is on the other foot,

God will also deal with them. Example: Let's say, Korah, Dathan, and Abiram were right and Moses was wrong. I believe God would have removed Moses. This is the other side of the story. He is a just God. When a member of the body of Christ has a concern, pastors should always listen, take it to the Lord in prayer and use God's word to settle it. You will never go wrong when using God's wisdom. We should not make assumptions when writing about pastor's honor having it appear that he is always right.

ARTICLE:

4. The Lord seemed to take it personal when the people spoke against the leader He appointed. Why? The writer believes the office of pastor is, in a sense, representative of God in the local church. Therefore the way we treat our pastor reveals some of our respect for God. When the church fails to honor the office of pastor – no matter who the person is – the church dishonors God.

MY RESPONSE:

4. God did take it personal when the people spoke out against the leader He appointed and I still believe God takes it personal. I've been told and have also read in cases such as this that God has stepped in and chastised people for conspiring to do wrong things against the pastor. I also believe God will step in when the pastor has gotten out of order by not dealing with Christians properly. Remember, leaders are human and make mistakes whether on purpose or not and they are accountable to God. Pastors are not

exempt from God's word if they get out of order. Pastors that are out of order happens more often then we believe.

Having concerns about a pastor who is doing things which are not representing God in the church is not dishonoring the office of pastor. Christians are protecting the office by making sure the pastor is not dishonoring it. The writer has no balance in his statements. It's always protecting the pastor and not the office. It's always blaming the people who have concern and not the leader. The pastor has a responsibility to make sure things are being done properly as Moses and Aaron did. God appoints people to the office of pastor to teach others the word which will help keep them on the right path to doing things God's way. The lack of honor doesn't always come from outside the office. There are always two sides to a story. The key is to have open discussions and let God say where the honor belongs.

ARTICLE:

5. To accuse and belittle a pastor without praying for him or her offends God, and when God is offended, the ground opens up to swallow the church's blessings, effectiveness and authority in the community. In other words, if we cannot honor the pastor whom we can see, how can we honor God whom we cannot see?

MY RESPONSE:

I agree if the pastor is being accused or belittled it does offend God. No one should do this. Pastors should not do this to anyone either. Dishonor in God's eye can come from anyone.

Pastor's should not conduct themselves in a way that would cause others to accuse or ridicule them and vice-versa. If the church is being operated according to His word, there is no room for concern. If this happens God will not be offended and the church will be blessed, effective, and an authority in the community. The statement to accuse and belittle the pastor without praying for him or her offends God. I agree, and when God is offended, the ground opens up to swallow the church's blessings, effectiveness, and authority in the community. If you believe this, what do you think will happen if the pastor offends the body of Christ?

If the leaders are looking for honor, I suggest they begin honoring God and doing things pastors should do (setting the example) as Christ did. Tell the whole story and don't play politics, but allow the Holy Spirit to control what is going on. I agree I can honor God without seeing Him (that's called faith). I also can honor His Son because of what He did and how He set His Father's standards for us to live by (that's also called faith). I can also honor His Holy Spirit that is within me as my guide and comforter (faith).

We are living in the human state and we can see what is going on. This makes it more difficult for pastors who should have the honor for their position God has given them. Evangelist Jim Baker was honored by many people, but lost that honor because of being dishonest. Maybe if people around him were praying and paying attention to what was going on or had asked God to give them knowledge and wisdom according to His word, perhaps he wouldn't have lost his honor. I wonder why the gift of discernment of spirits was not operating in anyone in the leadership. Did everyone just take Tammy and Jim for granted? It would probably blow our mind if we really knew how many of them are out there and no one is doing anything about it.

ARTICLE:

6. I believe a prayer hedge around the pastor honors him or her, because the highest honor you can give someone is to pray for them. And where honor is given, God will bestow victory and blessing. As a layperson, taking your pastor for granted is a sin! The reason a few opposers can harm a pastor is because the 95 percent of the congregation who like and support the pastor are not mobilized to pray for him or her. When you build a hedge of prayer around your pastor, you honor your pastor and you honor God.

MY RESPONSE:

6. I agree. But we first must make sure the pastor is not the cause of the problem. When the body of Christ prays and gets serious about becoming one, this will become the hedge around the pastor. The only way this will happen is to have open discussions without fear, paranoia, control and secrets. The people will have confidence in their leadership and the Holy Spirit will make sure things are being done in the proper way.

I suggest no one should take anyone for granted, it's a two way street. As I've stated, the pastor can be the problem and cause harm to the many in the congregation. I know of a pastor that did cause division because of his arrogant spirit against other people. I strongly believe that most church divisions are caused by a combination of ministers trying to keep their jobs (job security), causing them to become to political and over ambitious people (members of the church) who just want it their way. I believe it comes to one word—control. The pastor wants complete control and others would like to have that control, so it becomes a stale mate. The only one who wins in these cases is satan.

I have noticed, some men of God forget why God called them. They go off on tangents and then expect God to be pleased with them, and then don't understand why people get upset. In I Samuel 15 (KJV), Samuel anointed Saul and gave him instructions from the Lord. "Now go and strike Amalek and utterly destroy all they have and do not spare anyone; but put to death men and women, child and infant, ox and sheep, camel and donkey." God's command was clear. Saul was to wipe out this tribe forever. But, Saul's obedience to God was only partial. He won the battle, but failed to complete his instructions from God by capturing King Agag alive. Everything good they kept, everything worthless, they destroyed, whatever the reason. As a leader, he disobeyed the clear command of God. The sin that Saul committed as a leader was so serious that God immediately disposed of him and his descendents forever from the throne of Israel. He was rejected from ever being king. I am not sharing this story to instill fear in anyone, but to show that God is not a respecter of persons and there are two sides to every story. If Saul had just obeyed God, he would have been blessed in abundance. Because of God's grace some Christians think they are getting away with not obeying His commands. Wake up and read His word.

ARTICLE:

7. Jonathan Edwards (1703-1758), the famous early American preacher, once said: "if some Christians that had been complaining about their ministers had acted and said less before men and had applied themselves with all their might to cry to God for their ministers – had, as it were, risen and stormed heaven with their humble, fervent and incessant prayers for them- they would have much more in the way of success.

A pastor not prayed for is preyed on. The more a pastor threatens the enemy, the more severe will be the attack. But I believe God called your pastor to be fruitful. (John 15:8) Your shepherd needs to be fulfilled and happy in his or her work. Pastors need wisdom, anointing, rest, opportunities to share Christ, rich sermons, financial freedom, quality family time, a keen sense of fulfillment, realistic time management, vision and creativity. As a layperson, you are the key to lifting the pastor's battle-weary hands as Aaron and Hur lifted Moses' hands, keeping your pastor protected through all areas of ministry.

MY RESPONSE:

7. I agree 100%. Just remember it is a two way street. When reading this portion of the article it appears like these same things have been going on for many-many years. Who is to blame for this continuation of strife? I would strongly suggest the answer is in God's word. The church needs to stop practicing politics and start practicing God's way of doing things by everyone telling the truth. If pastors want

things to happen as happened to Moses and other great prophets of God and the honor that goes along with it, they should start listening to the Holy Spirit instead of man. I believe it's time to get serious, quit playing church, and start telling the truth about God's word. When the world compares Christianity with other religions and sees all the problems within, no wonder so many pick the other religions. The bottom line is, tell the truth, and stop playing politics. When this happens we might be surprised when all the people who left church start coming back and revival will breakout.

We should not confuse the Old Testament with the New Testament. God did things in the Old Testament under the Law that does not happen today under the new covenant, Grace. People in today's church do respect the pastor. After understanding God's word brought forth by the pastor and then seeing how things are being done, if not according to God's word, it is time for concern.

Moses was in a completely different situation. The Lord will take it personal today if someone speaks out against the pastor under the same circumstances as in Numbers 16 (KJV). Just a reminder, those people did not have God's word to study and understand how things should be done in the body of Christ. In those days, God spoke to individuals and not everyone. Today, God speaks to all who are born again through His Holy Spirit. Some Christian leaders have a difficult time accepting that fact. This has nothing to do with having respect or honor for the pastor. It has to do with listening to God as individuals. As a member of the body of Christ today, having concerns, God might ask you or me to address them, and you should get a response from the pastor and thank you from him for being concerned. All concerns about the body of Christ should be settled from God's word.

In today's Christian world, some leaders have the idea that they can use God's word to their advantage even though they might be out of God's will. God gave us His word to live by, not for pastors to threaten others with because of their own fear. We all belong to God. He's not a respecter of persons. In other words, He loves us all and expects us all to read and study His word to make ourselves approved. My concern is if we believe and teach God's word, have we, as Christians, used it as God says we should or do we only do it when pressured?

God wants us to treat people as His Son Jesus did, with love, and not use politics to try to control them. The Holy Spirit's responsibility is to guide us and He is in control, not the pastor. If people in the church get out of control according to God's word, He gives us ways in His word on how to deal with them. These standards and instructions come from the Holy Spirit for us to use when it is necessary. Matthew 18 is an excellent example. When using God's word to settle a dispute it will always turn out for the good of all.

The pastor is a representative of God, only a representative, not God. He or she must do as the Holy Spirit guides, through the word. After all, they are called by God. So, when people join Church, they expect leadership of the highest quality. They will respect the leadership that is following the word of God and if not, there is a concern, and they should be able to express and discuss the concern in an open forum, not in secret. If a pastor can not do this openly and defend his position because God placed him there, how does he expect people to respect him?

Another position we should respect and honor is the President of the United States. He is in a position of authority over our great Country. He has the same responsibility that a Pastor has, just much larger. He has many more people helping him then a Pastor has. They still have the responsibility for people. You've heard Presidents make the statement that he is responsible for the safety of the people of this Country. The problem with both positions is man with his ego can become corrupt. So we can always honor both offices, but not always the person that holds them.

I would like to share with you how churches are being operated compared to the Federal Government. I am not a political science major, but I'll give you my brief opinion of how our Government should work. There are three branches that Operate separately in our Governing system. There is the Executive Branch which administers the laws and handles the Government affairs. Next is the Legislative Branch which is made up of the House of Representatives and the Senate. The third is the Judicial Branch (Supreme Court) and these Judges administer Justice through the Courts. It has a check and balance system, which tries to keep everyone honest. The check and balance system is to make sure each branch of the Government don't get out of hand or take control. This system works fine as long as there is a balance. I've always believed the Supreme Court was not part of the political system, but recently I've changed my mind. Maybe I was just naive before. Our Government is getting out of control. Passing important bills that affect the people in the country without the Legislative Branch even reading or understanding what is in it is a sure indication of Government control. We are getting close to losing our freedom. Any politician that would make a statement about a bill "vote yes and read it later" without reading it first because they have control of the House and Senate is another indication of Government control. It blows my mind to think that same politician ran for re-election and got voted back in office. Our government system and the way people think is sick.

If all works like it should they should make sure the people in this Great Country are their first concern. There have been a few occasions (terrorist attacks) in the past when I don't think that has happened. I don't understand how everything works in Congress but I do understand how some of it worked in 2009 and the beginning of 2010. There was an imbalance of Politicians in Congress which allowed one political party to control and do as they please. So they took advantage as long as the imbalance was there. It was the worse group of Politicians that were elected by the people to represent the people that I've seen in my lifetime. This is a Country of fifty States, not two or three. Our Government should be treating them as equals. All of these politicians that get caught up in this bribery system from the President down through Congress should all be thrown out of office. If a citizen gets caught trying to bribe a police officer he would be locked up, go to trial, and a Judge would decide using the law whether he should spend time in jail. If the President or someone in Congress bribe each other that has to do with where our money goes, it's okay. I always thought bribery was bribery and illegal under the law.

They were not working for the people who elected them. They were only working for their particular political party and State. They were not being honest about the outcome of anything concerning the people and how it would affect them. Polls were taken on most things the White House and Congress wanted and the people indicated they did not want any of it, but they passed it anyway. This is the way it happens when one Political Party has control. This problem of giving away the store because the President just happens to be of the same political philosophy needs to stop. We need to get rid of the special interest groups and the lawyers and pay more attention to the people across this Country. We need to change the system so this doesn't happen again. They need to keep it balanced and both Parties need to remember who they are working for, the people. No closed door session, no secrets, no lies or out you go. Both political parties do the same thing when they are in power so the blame goes to both ways. The Independent party is looking better for the people who want things done right.

The way our system of Government should work is, these people are supposed to represent the people, not their political party. It is not working that way. One political party was in control and they left the other party out of their discussions and decision making. That continued until an election of one Senator that brought the system back into a balance. Anyhow, you can see how man gets out of control when the opportunity arises. This also shows how corrupt politicians can get when the system allows it. The only thing that stopped what was going on in our corrupt Government was the people across this beautiful country (Tea Parties) and in one particular State of Massachusetts. Thank God for the people that are starting to stand up for their rights.

THE CHURCH

This is how I believe the church is moving more towards the secular way of doing things.

How does this compare to the Government? God's church should have a check and balance system also. God's word says it should. This is where the secular world developed their system from, God's word. Churches are set up in a similar way. There is a Pastor (President), Board, Deacons/Elders (Congress), God's Word (Judicial). Of course the Denominational Organizations have a similar set up. The comparison to the Government is the church gets corrupt as well. I believe as long as man is in control the church will continue moving towards the secular way of doing things. The church leadership gets unbalanced and certain groups take control and do as they please. It gets to a point where the leadership doesn't really care about the people. I've seen this happen in two churches in recent years. The leadership becomes more like a dictatorship. The lies and deception like our Government has done in the past has become very evident in the church. Our churches are so full of politicians from top to bottom and we wonder why all the people have left the church.

The people in Massachusetts made sure in January of 2010 that the politicians understood they did not like how they were performing. The church should do the same. God's word says we Christians setting in the pews have a right to put a stop to any corruption we see in the church. The system will work if we will stand up and do what God's word says. I've seen it work in some churches. The word tells us we are allowed to test the Prophets (ministers). If we see something out of order or scriptures being misinterpreted we must not let it continue. Go to them and ask questions and share your concerns. If you get no answers or cooperation there are scriptures that tell you what to do. Look up Matthew 18 and study it. Just make sure your Christian walk is where it should be and if it's not, it will end up hypocrite against hypocrite.

MY PRAYER

God, break down the wall between ministers and laypeople that keep them apart. We all need to get back to the basics of how the body of Christ should function. We have drifted so far away from the true word that we can't see the trees for the forest. I pray that God will open our blind eyes before it's too late. A church without spot or wrinkle will take a lot of co-operation from both sides (yes both sides). I pray that the "body of Christ" will stop doing things that separate and cause them to always keep some of them at odds. I also pray that we stop blaming other's for sinning and not looking in the mirror at ourselves. Jesus said he who has not sinned, let him or her cast the first stone. I pray that the hypocrisy stops so the secular world sees it and wants to join the church. I pray this same prayer for our Federal Government, leaving it up to each individual and God on how to deal with it.

I BELIEVE As a Christian living under the laws of this Country that still gives everyone the freedom of free speech and religion I can attend the church of my choice. I want everyone to know I am not bowing down to another God by abiding by our Governments laws. God gave us this Christian Country and it is still standing for freedom around the word. I know our President says it is no longer a Christian Country but he needs to go back in History and read how our framers prayed and ask God for guidance. It was God that helped them through their trials and tribulations, not man. There might be other religions here in this country and they are welcomed, but we are still a Christian Nation and don't try to change that, it won't work. Making statements like the President made is nothing but political in nature and he knows that. We all know how politicians get votes, any way they can.

CHAPTER ELEVEN

JEZEBEL SPIRIT

My family and I attended a church a few years ago for a short period of time and we were very happy because God had impressed on us to go there. This was not a new church for us as we attended this church back in the late seventies/early eighties for a short period of time. This time we met some old and new Christian friends. We had stopped attending church for a period of time because God was showing us that churches were being overrun by people with political ambitions and if you tried to interfere you were black listed. My family and I had attended another church prior to this for many years and the congregation was slowly divided by fear and paranoia because politicians were always trying to control and take over and it eventually split the church. It did not take us long to understand this church was doing the same thing. People have never learned that it's God's church and He is in control, not man. Man is still depending on his own will by going down the road of disobedience. Ministers teach about God sending His Holy Spirit after the ascension of His Son Jesus to be with all Christians, to comfort and guide Christians until His return. The problem we humans have is we don't want to let go of the old man that was in us before salvation. The new man becomes a threat to mans ego. So the old man with his ego takes control and causes war between the two. Then they forget about God's will and direction by using their will to take control and guide everything.

I remembered a very close Christian friend sharing with me and others about a Jezebel spirit in this church. It had always been and would eventually be the demise of this ministry. I believe God sent me to this church to expose this Jezebel spirit and I believe I did. After reading a news letter from this church I concluded it was the biggest smoke screen I had ever seen or heard from two ministers. I eventually responded to the news letter because I believe the pastor had been conned by no one other then the Jezebel spirit. I will not share the entire news letter, but what I write here basically says the same thing as the letter with added emphasis. It all has to do with exposing a Jezebel spirit. I thanked the Pastor for the copy of the church news letter. We as a family was glad that he sent this copy to update us on Jezebel, "accuser of the brethren" EXPOSED. I hoped this was not another smokescreen which we normally see when someone is trying to cover something up.

The Jezebel spirit is in most churches and it will stay unless the people stop playing church politics and start using what God made available for us to rid the church of this bad spirit. Christians need to become more serious about spiritual things, and remove the bad spirit, but not the person unless absolutely necessary. The person with this spirit needs to admit having it, ask God for forgiveness, take charge of it, and remove it from their life in the name of Jesus Christ. The Jezebel spirit is a form of the religious spirit. Just as Jezebel was the ambitious and manipulating wife of King Ahab, a weak leader who allowed her to dictate policy in his kingdom, the Jezebel spirit will usually be found supplanting weak leadership. The Jezebel spirit is manipulative and usually gains it's dominion by making political alliances, often in a seemingly submissive and demanding manner. However once this spirit gains authority, it will usually manifest a strong control spirit and shameless presumption.

Jezebel "calls herself a prophetess" (Rev. 2:20 KJV). This is often one of the telltale signs of false prophets who are operating in a religious spirit. They are preoccupied with their own recognition. They are corrupted to the degree that self-seeking and the need for recognition abides within them. Jezebel demands recognition for herself while serving as the enemy of the true prophetic ministry. Jezebel was the greatest enemy of one of the old covenant's most powerful prophets, Elijah, whose ministry especially represents preparing of the way for the Lord. The Jezebel spirit is one of the most potent forms of the religious spirits which seeks to keep the church and the world from being prepared for the return of the Lord. This spirit will make us feel very good about our spiritual condition as long as it is self-centered and self-seeking. Pride feels good; it can even be exhilarating, but it keeps all of our attention on how well we are doing, on how we stand compared to others, not on the glory of God. If God is showing you a person that fits this description you'll know He is talking to you.

There is forgiveness and deliverance from this Jezebel spirit, but first it has to be recognized and I believe some pastors have begun that journey in recognizing that their church has a Jezebel spirit indwelling. Continue to search and pray for your eyes to be opened so your church can finally be free to go forward down the path God set out for it.

An excellent book other than the Bible for information on the Jezebel spirit is, Epic Battles of the Last Days by Rick Joyner. If you're reading this book, please read it with an open mind and an open heart which will put the necessary balance in your Christian walk. It has truly been an eye-opening book with much confirmation on what God asked me to expose.

I believe this particular church we were attending had a very strong Jezebel spirit and God allowed me to identify it. The problem with this Jezebel spirit is, it had a close relationship with many in the church, including family. The reason I believe most churches have this spirit is because none of the Spirit filled Christians have used the gift for discerning bad spirits. All they want to do is play church and politics. They are not using God's gifts listed in Cor.12 (KJV). Some churches use one or two but are lacking balance by not using them all. I believe some have misinterpreted how to use them and are doing the same as the original churches. Read the Epistles where Paul had to address the churches about many things including being out of order. In some churches today they prophesy over each other (personal) interrupting the message from God (not scriptural). Christians have gradually moved away from belonging to the body of Christ and everything being about God to being all about "me".

We stopped making sure ministers are teaching the truth. This particular Jezebel has been active for many years and because of relationships within the church it stays and has become strong and will cause the slow demise of the church. If you are a Christian that likes to play politics you will never recognize this spirit. If you're serious about serving God and you believe His gifts are for Christians today, use them all as indicated in 1Cor.12 (KJV) and the body of Christ will become balanced. Ministers should always teach about the body of Christ and how it should function. If all this is done according to God's word there will be no Jezebel spirits or politicians trying to control things in your church. Politics and control is the name of the game that keeps the Jezebel spirit alive and active.

To make a long story short my questions and concerns about many things happening in the church caused a short stay for me and my family again. We were forced to leave because I was asking too many questions about things that the leadership didn't like. After leaving we continue to receive the church news letter. We received a news letter concerning a Jezebel spirit being exposed. Sense we had just left the church it appeared like they were pointing the finger in my direction, maybe not. I was the one voicing my concerns about things being out of order in the church. I didn't completely agree with some of the others about their concerns, but listened and discussed their concerns with them because the leadership didn't want to talk with them.

It appeared to me that some of these others wanted to share or take over the ministry. They shared with me visions they said were from God, but, they never came to fruition. I would like to share how I responded to some of the news letter.

I will not share all the comments made by two ministers in this news letter, but give a brief written overview to what I believe God was showing me how to respond to what they were saying.

News letter:

The Lord Jesus Christ wants to see the demon spirit of the accuser of the brethren stamped out of the thought process of the church.

My response:

I agree!! It appears as though you finally want to lead the church in the right direction. It's about time the church people stand up and become responsible to protect the body of Christ. It always appeared as though the church never wanted to address the Jezebel spirit. I pray that politics aren't played when a demon is exposed within the church. In God's word there are no exceptions. On the human level it's always the other person violating God's principles and never the prophet, pastor, or teacher, etc. Only telling one side of a story usually comes from someone trying to protect themselves from being exposed. This is the secular political way of doing it. Most politicians don't tell the whole story for personal reasons. They want to stay in power so they tell lies. The same thing is happening in our churches.

When telling stories to describe something about God's word, we should study them very carefully before sharing them with the congregation. We should never let our mouth get ahead of our mind or our heart. Concerns and what some would consider accusations of people if true in the body of Christ might be good for all. This is how we learn. If all communications are interpreted in the wrong way it will put people in a position to defend them-selves. If you just want to protect yourself or someone close to you or convince people they are wrong in everything they say, God will not allow that. I believe God was in everything that happened, because it finally is exposing the Jezebel spirit that's had its' way for all these years. Whether you will admit it or not, God knows some come as a help to you and your ministry and not as a troublemaker.

News letter:

The Jezebel assault is on all levels; families, churches, and inter-church associations. Masquerading as discernment slips into our opinions of other people.

Response:

I agree!! This should never happen if the Holy Spirit is in control. Jezebel spirits do spread gossip and have an opinion about everyone and aren't afraid to say they know their tongue gets them into trouble, but the demon has control so they continue with the gossip. I know of people who confess this, but continue for years and the church never deals with it. I agree a gossiping tongue destroys God's church and vision. These statements in your news letter should have opened your eyes many years ago.

News letter:

God does answer prayer.

Response:

Now that you have opened your eyes as indicated by this message to the people, I pray that you take the next biblical step and that should be to cast out that demon in the name of Jesus from your midst. As I have shared with you the Jezebel spirit has been in your church from the beginning. I don't quite understand why such a long period of time had to pass before you finally decided to address the demon. I also do not understand why it took someone else to write about it before you decided to share it. The author of the book you read apparently understands God's word. It should not take a minister thirty to forty years to determine he has a Jezebel in the church. It didn't take this amount of time to know you must ask God for forgiveness of your sins to be born again or to use God's gifts. Blaming others for problems in the church is wrong. When doing this you are joining the jezebel spirit.

Quite a few years ago a Christian with the gifts of wisdom and knowledge saw that same spirit and was afraid to mention it because of relationships within the church. Others in the church today see the same Jezebel spirit and are afraid to talk about it. Why? It's because of the mom and pop syndrome and not wanting to hurt or upset the applecart or hurt somebody's feelings. This is the wrong way God wants His people to react to a bad spirit in the body of Christ. These people will slowly come to a conclusion that the jezebel spirit is still there and they will leave the church instead of confronting it and demanding it to leave in the name of Jesus. Some Christians set people up on a pedestal instead of Jesus, putting their eyes on the wrong one. They are more interested in their political relationships in the church than they are pleasing their Father by accepting changes that He wants to make in the church and in them. I thank God for using me to help expose the accuser of the brethren.

It was shared with me by a church leader that a Jezebel spirit was among the congregation in your church. This was revealed (conformation) to the leader from your church at a Christian conference. The minister at the conference did not identify who the Jezebel was, but your church leader did put a name to the person the spirit was on, when sharing it with me. The leader told me who it was and this person was eventually removed from the church. Maybe the minister at the conference was confused or afraid to say who the Jezebel was. I believe the minister should have, because it sounded like God's Spirit was really moving. It seemed kind of odd to me that the minister at the conference that revealed the Jezebel, but didn't give a name, and the church leader knew who it was. If this leader knew in advance who it was, why didn't he/she go to the minister at the church and cast out the Jezebel, it's scriptural. The leader didn't say to me that

God revealed the persons name, but said they knew who it was.

Some of this might be confusing to the readers of this book, but believe me the leaders in this particular church are blind to what has and still is going on. This letter was probably written in 2002/03 and I believe the Jezebel spirit continued to do what they do, control people.

CHAPTER TWELVE

CULTISM AND OCCULTS

I never believed studying about cults was necessary until I was exposed to a newspaper article being shared by a local church minister during a church service. The article was written by another local minister about what he believed happened in Waco, Texas. I believe the reading of this article and response by the congregation was out of order in a church service and was not Christian like when people can't defend themselves. Reading this from a news paper article and not explaining who it was written by is not letting the people know whether it was a right or left political opinion. It was like being in a political meeting where people were only interested in one side of the story. This religious group (cult) led by David Karish was using occult ways to operate a closed system. It was a cult with secret and mysterious motives and would not let the public be involved in what they were doing in the fortress they built. It was an incident between the Federal Government and a religious group that ended in a tragedy with many people losing their lives. I always thought in any religion a cult was a group of people lead by someone that had taken scripture out of context (to the extreme) and lead people down the wrong path using occultism as their system of belief. Some religious cults using occult methods end by the people dying for no reason. They usually die because of some crazy person with his/her hidden agenda. They take advantage of people who are gullible enough to believe their lies. This has happened many times in this country. Others cults of this nature exist and continue to flourish because there is no effort by the mainstream churches to get them on the right path. This is when the government gets into the act especially when there are young children involved. If you did an extensive study on each major Denomination you would probably find cults that branched off from each one. Some are not as extreme as others, but the Government still keeps tabs on them and they should.

Article and my opinion:

I believe this article originated or was used by a minister who I believe had completely taken certain scriptures out of context. He was trying to gain sympathy from others in the area for his dispute with the local government concerning taxes and signing a specific document for the government which gives the church the right to become tax exempt. By signing this document he believes he would be serving two Masters and the Bible teaches against that. He is correct about serving two Masters and Christians should not do that. He is trying to show that "big government" is in control of everything. By doing this he believes we will be serving two Masters. His only problem is he signs everything the government requires except this particular document. The material in this letter has to do with defending his case on not paying taxes on a building he was using for a church. His reason for using the government is another way of trying to prove his point of explaining why he was not paying his taxes or signing the document. He says to partake of men's private system and pay the taxes due therefore is to support a government bent on destroying God's dominion (meaning Waco Texas). If he is including the Waco compound as God's dominion he needs to re-read God's word. He goes on to say, this is from "an enemy of God responsible for murdering our brothers, sisters and children at Waco Texas". He then goes on to say according to the government statement, if you are a follower of Christ, you are an enemy of the government. This quote is in response to the question, why the killing of the people of Waco Texas was necessary. The answer may shock you, he says. The "reason" for murdering them, said "the government ", was because they were cultist.

I read Webster's dictionary and this is how it defines cultism: "a system of religious worship or ritual. The term religious is characterized by adherence to religion or a religion. Ritual is characterized as a set form or system of rites (like dancing). This person said during the Waco incident the Attorney General's explanation was, "a cultist is one who has a strong belief in the Bible and the second coming of Christ. One who frequently attends Bible studies and who has a high level of financial giving to a Christian cause. One who home schools for their children and accumulates survival foods and has a strong belief in the 2nd amendment and distrust big government. The Attorney General then says, any of these may qualify a person as a cultist, but certainly more than one of these would cause us to look at this person as a threat, and his family as being in a risk situation that would qualify for government interference. Notice the Attorney General said "may qualify", meaning, the possibility exist. I guess if he is correct in quoting the Attorney General the government should investigate all groups that are doing weird things like the people at Waco and Guiana and I would agree. If he means the Attorney General should investigate all churches, I don't think so.

I guess you could say the dictionary and the Government consider all religious groups a possible cult. Anyhow after hearing this discussion I ask the minister if I could make some comments on the subject, and he said yes. I thanked him for allowing me to address the subject. I've said to some people over the years when sharing things with others, one should know the whole story and tell it in its' fullest content. By doing this, one will not fall into the trap of having people saying Amen or making negative comments about a story that might not deserve it, which the congregation did. During the reading of the letter by the pastor there were very negative comments from others about one person's health. This was all uncalled for because only one paragraph of the article was read. Even though only a portion was read, the response from some in the congregation did not show a Christian like attitude. The correct response should have been to pray for this person, not laugh, and pick fun of ones affliction. I am sure God was not pleased with that response from His people. It is very easy for Christians to fall into the thinking pattern of the secular world.

I told the Pastor what I have to say is constructive criticism, only to show how we can get into trouble by what we say and what we don't say. Please don't misunderstand what I'm going to say about the disaster in Waco, TX. I have never read the official report about the whole incident so what I have to share is what I read in the news paper or seen on television. I believe there were many mistakes made by both sides. So let us not blame or accuse one side of murdering innocent people because they just happened to work for the Government, especially when this discussion came about by a minister who despises the Government. This person does not think they should sign a peace of paper to give them a tax free status. Their justification is, it would make them submit to Government rule and this would cause them to serve two masters. So all he wants to do is get others to believe him and be against the government in all things.

This entire incident could have been stopped by one individual by the name David Karish. I believe he is the one who gave the order to fire their guns at people outside the building, and he would not let some of the people leave. Let's not overlook what was reported to the authorities about what was happening inside the structure. I believe there were some people outside of the compound that had serious concerns about what David Karish was doing, and I think it had to do with young girls. Even if he was not involved with young girls, I still don't believe any parent would want their daughter or any member of their family involved, not knowing what was really going on inside of the compound. How many of these type religious cults have we seen end up in a disaster where people end up dead.

There are more details to the story, but lets continue on the subject.

As I recall, in the past there were certain religious groups listed as cults which closely match the Attorney Generals explanation. I will only mention a few such as, the people in Guyana (a religious group that committed suicide), a religious group in the west who waited in their beds to be taken away at the return of Christ (committing suicide), probably because someone in their group gave a prophecy on the time of His return and we know that is not biblical truth. Both of these incidents were caused by religious individuals and not by individuals in the Government. This same thing appears to have happened in another religious group in Waco, Texas. I believe there are many other religious cults the Government needs to keep an eye on, like the Pentecostals down South who worship in snake handling. I believe some Protestants view Catholicism as a cult, as do the Catholic's view some of the Protestants denominations as a cult.

I believe any church can be accused of being a cult if they don't make sure they are teaching the truth about God's word which means proper interpretations. IF YOU CAN'T PROVE IT BY GOD'S WORD THE CHURCH SHOULD NOT BE DOING IT. There are too many personal interpretations of the word and used by some and accepted by others that end up getting them into trouble, like in the compound at Waco, TX. This is why I believe it is very important for the church to test all prophesy and interpretations of GOD'S word. If this is not done the cults will continue to pop up in the future. The mainline churches, Catholic and Protestant alike are having enough trouble dealing with problems because they kept evil a secret. I believe the Minister's explanation in this article is completely wrong for blaming the Government for what happened in Waco, TX.

My response is, IF YOU BELIEVE THAT THE GOVERNMENT WOULD PURPUSELY KILL MEN, WOMEN, AND CHILDREN BECAUSE THEY ARE CLASSIFIED AS CULTISTS, YOU ARE VERY MISINFORMED. What I suggest, before you make statements such as are in the letter, you need to do your homework and ask God to confirm who is right or wrong and not try to use this for your defense. The people inside the compound being blind to the truth lost their lives because the leader was leading them down the wrong path. He was satan incarnate as far as I'm concern. The reason why the leader was keeping the government out was because he knew they would restrain him. He knew he might be put in prison for the crimes he was committing. I guess when you're looking for ways to help your cause you'll try anything, like this minister has done in this article. His only aim was to try and convince the people the government is out to kill all Christians especially if they don't pay their taxes or sign a certain document. I believe until Christ returns the government is the restrainer of evil even if there is some evil in the government. If the government fails to restrain evil, especially in this Country, who will? This country has always led the way in helping other countries gain their freedoms and restrain evil. If the government in our country allows things to continue after being advised by the public about evil happenings within a so called church compound, the people in general would be in an uproar.

The Catholic Church has kept secrets about pedophiles for years and look at the outcome. They lost control but didn't want the government to get involved. They will slowly release the pedophiles and it now becomes the responsibility of the general public and government. The problem with this is the church didn't want the responsibility to begin with. These people would still be getting away with what others would be put in jail for if it wasn't for our Government Justice system. Is this the system we want or do we want someone helping the church in a positive way? The Protestant churches are involved in similar things, catching leaders (pastors) who are not only robbing the church, but, are hypocrites and probably not even called by God, and now it is the homosexual problem. Just remember, if you remove the government, who will slip in and take control? There is not enough unity and structure in the church [THE BODY OF CHRIST] at this time to deal with all the evil that's going on in our society today, so I'm glad the government is available even though there are many evil things going on within their ranks.

CHAPTER THIRTEEN

PROPHETS AND PROPHCY

I attended local Pentecostal churches from an infant to 2009 and was exposed to all that happens during their church services. I was never exposed to what some Southern Pentecostal churches do by handling snakes which I believe is a complete misinterpretation of God's word. This is what I consider a cult. While growing up in this church I was taught their doctrine and believed what they were saying to be the truth. When I was in my twenties the Holy Spirit started showing me certain things they were doing was not matching God's word that I was reading. Again this is not pointing the finger, it's sharing what God has showed me and I would like to share this with all Christians.

In this chapter I would like to share with you what I was taught and seen happen in Pentecostal churches about prophets and prophecy. Some material includes other Protestant and Catholic churches. Some churches disagree with the use of God's gifts mentioned in 1Cor. 12 (KJV) are for our use today. I would like to say I disagree with them, but would agree in certain circumstances because some Christians abuse and fake their use and some misuse them. I will try to help you understand what I mean.

Before I go into what I believe about prophets and prophecy, let us take a look at what God says about Spiritual Gifts and especially prophecy. The Gifts are given by God and Him only. All gifts mentioned in God's word are of a supernatural nature because only God can give them. His Holy Spirit is in charge of distribution to who He please. Being called by God to be a prophet today is not the same as the Old Testament prophets. They did declare and predict by the influence of God. They also preached and taught about God the Father. Being able to prophesy (predict/teach) is a divine gift from God. Spiritual gifts of the Holy Spirit are supernatural, not natural. To give a prophecy is to predict the future and is always under the influence of God. That is what the prophets did in the Old Testament. Giving a prophecy is not a natural talent that you possess. Some people today call themselves prophets and even attend prophet seminars. They make the Bible say what they want it to say. They use their interpretation of scriptures to support their position instead of letting the scriptures speak for themselves.

When understanding Acts 6, the apostles finally understood that they were not to get involved with the daily operation of the church. Their responsibility was to study and teach the Word of God. I observed a few pastors over the years who were more involved in the daily administration of the church that they lost people due to the lack of study and teaching. This is sometimes caused by fear and paranoia on their part. I also have seen the opposite where a pastor studied all the time and had an outstanding teaching, but again would not trust others to take the administrative part of the church. I believe this was also caused by fear and paranoia. Trust was lacking in both cases. I believe what is missing here is the lack of understanding that the Bible needs to be read and studied more frequent than other books so the truth can be taught. The Holy Spirit came to lead and guide us in all truth. He is the Spirit of truth and the only one available to us that knows the mind of God. God spoke to the people in the Old Testament through the prophets and in the New Testament through the apostles. Some ministers will say there are no more apostles in our church today because they consider there were only twelve and after their death there were no more. We end up with prophets, missionaries, pastors and teachers. I believe any teacher of God's word today is an apostle. They are not at the same level as the original apostles, because they were considered foundational. Jesus is the cornerstone and the apostles built the foundation and started the church. Today there are no foundational apostles, not needed. What we have today is pastors, evangelist, missionaries, teachers etc. Keep in mind we are all suppose to be like apostles when we accept Jesus Christ as our Savior. We are supposed to go out, share the gospel, and bring sinners in. It's called winning souls for God.

I BELIEVE: WHEN DEFINING AN OFFICE FILLED BY GOD'S CALLING, AN APOSTLE, EVANGILIST, PROPHET, PASTOR, AND TEACHER ARE SIMILAR IN NATURE. THEY ALL TEACH THE WORD OF GOD.

THE PASTOR HAS AN ADDED RESPONSIBILITY, BECAUSE THEY BECOME THE SHEPHERD OF THE FLOCK.

There is a vast difference between the Old and New Testament prophets. Some try to give the New Testament prophet the same status as the Old Testament prophet, but they are not the same. In the Old Testament God gave the prophets revelations for His word (A revelation is the revealing or disclosing of something, a thing not previously known). They were the only ministers anointed by God for preaching and teaching the people. I'm not saying God wouldn't do it now because he is God and can do as He pleases. I'm saying I haven't seen any prophecies as was given in the Old Testament in church today. Remember what the definition is (a thing not previously known). Most of what you hear today is predictions from mans intellect.

If all these so called prophets in this country and around the world would spend as much time doing what God said, perfect the saints (teach them the word), for the work of the ministry (send them out to minister to the sinner), and edifying the body of Christ (build them up, which means to give moral and spiritual instruction and help them improve) the church of Christ would be much stronger. In the New Testament it is not scriptural for prophets to give revelations. Remember, we can not add to or take away from His Word, IT IS COMPLETE. This is what happens when some people deceive others into believing they get revelations from God, such as the Mormon, Muslim and Jehovah Witness. Even Mohammad decided he got a revelation because he didn't like the way things were written in the Bible so he started teaching Muslims what eventually was written in the Koran. If you don't like what is being said from God's word change it to suit yourself. The same thing happened with these other religions. This is still happening in our churches today, only telling one side of the story. Jesus set the five fold ministry in the church for the perfecting of the saints (Eph. 4:11-12 KJV). The people Jesus appoints to these offices now must follow His commands, they are not to lead or guide, but to serve, teach and instruct others how to win souls for Christ. The Holy Spirit will do the guiding.

I believe some Old Testament type prophets and there were about thirty nine people spoken of as prophets in the Old Testament. John the Baptist and Zacharias are the last of the Old Testament type prophets listed in the Gospels in the New Testament. These prophets were a primary type prophet. God picked these men to be His mouth piece. I know there are other scriptures saying there were other prophets, but, I believe they were secondary prophets. There were secondary prophets mentioned in 1Cor. 12:28 and Eph. 4:11(KJV). They are given God's gifts along with evangelist, pastors and teachers to edify the Body of Christ, not make predictions about the future. I believe God has already done that from Genesis through Revelation. So, we can't add to or take away from His written word, it is complete. Read De. 4:2, 12:32, Pr. 30:6 (KJV). When Jesus was crucified and ascended back to the Father, He sent His Holy Spirit to fill the gap until His return. The Holy Spirits arrival started the New Testament times on the day of Pentecost. I know there were other prophets mentioned (not by name) in the Old Testament, but, they were not predicting the future. John the Baptist and Zacharias were the last to make predictions about the future. Jesus was regarded as a prophet but his assignment was to teach Gods word to his disciples and send them out to preach and teach the gospel. He was given all authority from the Father to use all spiritual gifts. Jesus gave partial authority to His disciple also to use the gifts. The law was abolished as it says in Luke 16:16 (KJV); "The law and the prophets were until John: Sense that time, the Kingdom of God is preached and every man presseth into it". It is talking about "ceremonial law". "Until John" means he was the last Old Testament type prophet. Jesus was the New Testament King, Priest and Prophet.

It says in Eph. 4:8-12 (KJV), "When He (Jesus) ascended up on high He lead captivity captive, and gave gifts unto men, and He (Jesus) gave some, apostles, and some, prophets, and some, evangelists, and some, pastors and teachers." In 1Cor. 12:28 (KJV), it starts out by saying "And God has set some in the church." My point here is man has nothing to do with calling anyone to an office. I do believe the Roman Church squashed God's way of doing the calling as they did other things especially during the Inquisition period. It is a divine call from God. Also, every person called is subject to the same qualifications stated in 1Tim.3 (KJV). If someone claims to be a prophet and you don't know them or their background and you're not using the gift of discernment to test the message and messenger, BEWARE. How many so called prophets have been tested by God's word that you know? I have only seen one so called prophet or prophecy tested in any Pentecostal church I attended over the years. I know you will say I am wrong because you know of prophets today that make predictions about the future and some come true. If some so called prophet makes predictions and only some happen, they are not prophets. If the message is from God it will come to past. People that call themselves prophets have very good backgrounds through study or experience in what they make predictions about and this can fool people. God gives the prophet through His Holy Spirit what is to be said and it will happen. When you give a prophecy and nothing happens, you make God a liar. People that do this will weaken the Christian testimony. I've seen this happen in small and mega churches that are broadcasting around the world. I believe there are about one thousand prophecies in God's word and about five hundred of them have already been fulfilled. We have forgotten what we should be doing according to God's word. Evangelizing the world is our assignment. That is why Jesus taught the twelve apostles for three years. If someone in a service gives a message, it is for edification and the building up of the body of Christ. This is not a prophecy it is a word of wisdom and knowledge for edification.

The people that God chooses to give His gifts to will use them for the perfecting of the saints, for the work of the ministry, and for the edifying of the body of Christ. During my studies concerning the gifts mentioned, I have concluded that the office of apostle only lasted until all of the original apostles were gone. Changes were made by the church over the years to not use some of these gifts. Why? Probably because people abused the gift God gave them. I believe the so called prophets continued in the office of preacher which was God's spokesperson to particular times, cultures and situations. Evangelists traveled from place to place with the gospel announcing the good news of Jesus Christ. They were followed by pastors and teachers or pastor-teacher, who then nurtured the flock. Some Pastors could do the work of evangelist (2Tim. 4:5 KJV).

My Christian experience with how the church has justified so called prophets and prophecy over the years is because the gift of discerning of spirits is never used. The reason, there is a spirit of fear in control among the people belonging to the body of Christ. Most people are afraid to speak up when the Holy Spirit is telling them the message and the messenger is false. Also Pentecostals like to push the gift of tongues and prophecy, but never question what is being said, or follow up on whether it was edifying to the body of Christ, or just an emotional speech. Anyhow, I don't see anything it has done for the church in terms of edification, exhortation, and comfort, and it does not appear to have done anything for church unity. Man is still trying to control everything done in the church, and are still far apart on their doctrines and no one seems concerned about it. If we Christians continue to live with different beliefs about God's word how do we ever expect to be in unity? The question is who is telling the truth? Churches have been failing, some closing and locking their doors, and some with just a handful of people because man was and is still in control instead of God. Just remember God gave us a will and as long as we want control he will let us have it.

I believe that most spiritual gifts being used today are coming from individuals with intellectual and not spiritual knowledge. These people have big egos and like to impress others. It's called pride and self-edification which in our society today is called building our self esteem. We need to understand the different personalities because it always appears as though one certain type (red/politician) is always speaking in unknown tongues (true or not?), giving the interpretation or giving a prophecy. This is not always the case, but, I would venture to say, most of the time it is. God is not a respecter of persons. He doesn't care who you are, how intelligent, or how much money you have. He chooses who he wants to give a message to the church and could care less about personalities. His twelve apostles were a diverse group with different personalities and levels of intellect, but, all received the Gift of tongues on the day of Pentecost. When God gives a message to the church, He does it in His time and not in some politician's time. You know every time they attend church or any Christian function the red personality shows up wanting to see themselves (build their ego), so they give what everyone believes is a message from God. I believe what I've seen most of the time concerning the gifts over the years is fake, not scriptural, and out of order. When Christians are approached about this they are afraid to discuss it because they might be caught up in a false doctrine.

This has been my observation in many Pentecostal churches over the years and it always happened this way. When someone receives the gift of salvation there was always jubilation. You could always see it in their eyes and the smile on their face. They want to share this experience with everybody they meet. This is a miracle that happens at salvation and should cause a feeling of jubilation. If it doesn't there is something wrong. I have also seen this when someone is slain in the spirit. Being filled to overflowing with God's Spirit will make you dance, laugh, sing, to show the new born again person in you. You can no longer see that old person, he steps out and the new person steps in. I have always questioned why I never see this happen with any of the other gifts. Why don't this happen with other supernatural gifts like prophecy, discernment of spirits, knowledge and wisdom etc. Paul said prophecy is more important? The gift of love according to Paul is more important than all the other gifts. I believe Paul came down hard on the Corinthian church for doing the same as the church is doing today, abusing the gifts. Another observation is there are some people that don't take their salvation very serious. All the people that I have seen over the years when praying the sinner's prayer have always shown a change in their countenance, no matter the personality type. When God forgives you of your sins and you become a new man in Christ you can't help from being jubilant. I don't see this in many people today that claim they accepted Jesus Christ as their savior.

Under the New Covenant, we Christians are to follow the Holy Spirit guidance for ourselves (Rom. 8:14 KJV). This Holy Spirit was given to us because of the atonement by God's Son. Under the Old Covenant, there was a sacrificial system for worship because God was dealing with spiritually dead people. They couldn't worship God in spirit and truth, WE CAN. In the Old Testament only those whom God chose had the Holy Ghost upon them. In the New Testament, if we believe in God and accept His Son Jesus Christ as our Savior the Holy Spirit enters in to comfort and guide us. We become spiritually alive. It is entirely up to us how we live our lives. We have to decide whether or not we want to live a Christian life. The Holy Spirit is only there to guide and help if asked.

Under the Old Covenant the only people who were spiritually anointed by God were the prophets, priest and kings. Out of these the Prophet was the only one that was anointed to preach. The layman was not anointed because they were spiritually dead. In the New Testament it says "For as many as are led by the Spirit of God, they are the Sons of God" (Rom. 8:14 KJV). Under the Old Covenant people couldn't be led by their spirits, and they couldn't approach God for themselves. In the Old Testament, the people didn't have the Holy Ghost to lead and guide them, so they went to the prophet to inquire what "Thus saith the Lord".

Under the New Covenant, prophets (pastors) were not called to this office to lead and guide. We have the Holy Spirit to lead and guide us. Put your trust in God, not man. This is one of the problems in the church today. We allow man to lead and guide us knowing this is not scriptural. By doing this the Holy Spirit steps aside because of our free will. Instead of allowing the Holy Spirit to guide and lead us in the right direction man continues to believe he can do a better job, but continues to flounder. Instead of pastors staying in their assignment, they want to do everything, like manage the building affairs, lead and guide peoples lives, raise money and develop gimmicks for increasing membership. If the membership fades he starts taking the peoples money for his personal benefit and not the church, etc. They need to spend their time studying the word to make sure the truth is being told and follow the Holy Spirits guideline instead of just taking the word of some denominational belief. Educating the body of Christ and preparing the people for soul winning (done by setting the example) is more important.

REMEMBER, WE CAN GO STRAIGHT TO THE FATHER, BECAUSE WE HAVE HIS SPIRIT IN US. WE ARE SPIRITUALLY ALIVE AND HE WILL GUIDE US BY HIS HOLY SPIRIT, NOT A PROPHET. IF GOD TALKS TO ONE ABOUT FILLING AN OFFICE, WHY WOULDN'T GOD TALK WITH ALL ABOUT WHAT HE WANTS THEM TO DO? HE WILL!

It is unscriptural to allow a so called prophet of today do the leading and guiding. He did this in the Old Testament because they (primary prophets) were the ones He put His Spirit upon. In the New Testament His Spirit is upon all born again Christians. Normally a believer will be led by the Holy Spirit through his own spirit. God may speak through a prophet (secondary) or any believer as a confirmation to another person for something they already know. This is not leading or guiding. This is only giving a conformation, not a prophecy.

We as "Sons of God" can be expected to be led by the Spirit of God, so the number one way the Holy Spirit leads us, including a prophet (pastor), is by the inward witness. The Holy Spirit leads by the still small voice. Believers are led by the authoritative voice of the Holy Ghost in their own spirit. Based upon better promises (Heb. 8:6 KJV), we don't need to seek direction for our own lives from anyone but God. Jesus is our High Priest. The Holy Spirit is our comforter and guide.

Jesus' blood obtained eternal redemption for us (Heb. 9:12KJV) and being born again, we are led by the Holy Spirit in our own spirit. Under the New Covenant we are made Kings and Priests unto God (1 Pet. 2:9, Rev. 5:9-10 KJV). All believers have access to God themselves. That is why Jesus died on the cross. We are not required to go through the Pope, Priest, Prophet, Pastor, Apostle etc., only Jesus! If you're not listening to God, but taking advice and guidance from a so called prophet, you better ask God if this is right or wrong. Just remember the deceiver!!! False prophets (pastors/teachers)!!!!

I recently read an article about a school where they are teaching people how to become healers. I'm sure there are prophet schools also. Where in the New Testament does the scripture say anything about this? The gift of healing is just that, a gift given by God, not man. Jesus appoints those whom He wants to work His healing according to His will, not ours. Let us not confuse the Old Testament prophet schools developed by Samuel with the New Testament ways in which God wants to teach people. Remember, Samuel was a prophet with the Holy Ghost upon him. His students could not go straight to the Father as we can, so Samuel was teaching them how to be teachers. Teachers, prophets, pastors, and evangelists are pretty much the same and require the same qualifications listed in 1Tim.3 (KJV).

In Eph. 4:12 (KJV), it says God gave us leaders to help perfect the saints, for the work of the ministry, and for the edifying of the body of Christ. In V13 it says the leaders are to do this until we all come in the unity of faith, and of the knowledge of the son of man, unto the measure of the stature of the fullness of Christ. I do believe the church has failed in this respect. Today, everyone wants to get in the act of leadership, going off on their own tangent and not sticking to and following the word of God. I would like to ask a lot of ministers if God called them or were they appointed by man. Remember in the Old Testament prophets spoke for God and not themselves. (Jeremiah 1:4-8 KJV). Another example is found in Isaiah 6:1-1-3 (KJV).

John the Baptist was an Old Testament prophet but never used the phrase "thus saith the Lord". He did make predictions such as the coming of the Mighty One, Jesus. Jesus was a prophet and made many predictions. His predictions were to fulfill prophecies and God's plan. You'll find many prophecies in the New Testament, but mostly predictions that had already been made in the Old Testament.

The gifts, including prophecy were given to all believers at Pentecost (Acts 2:1-21 KJV). These same gifts were used by chosen ones in the Old Testament. They were given to fulfill God's word as stated in the Book of Joel. They were given for proper use through the Holy Spirit and not used for our personal benefit in any way. Prophets and laymen in

New Testament times are to share events in the divine plan. God's gifts are being misused in the Body of Christ today as was done in the Corinthian Church as Paul pointed out.

Last but not least, the false prophet. His message frequently appealed to pride and still does today. His message is usually spurred by self interest and given to please people. Most prophecies given are in error. Jesus warned His disciples that false Christ will arise, and try to deceive God's elect.

The bottom line here is I believe prophets today should be teaching the word of God and quit spending so much time on their ego and edifying themselves. Leave the guiding of peoples lives up to the HOLY SPIRIT. These so called prophets are going around feeding on each others egos. Having conferences for so called prophets is stretching it. It's like the minister sharing with a Bible study group in my home saying he and other ministers met frequently and practiced speaking in tongues and giving prophecies. That is really stretching God's patients. Does this say anything about man wanting and taking control?

CHAPTER FOURTEEN

GIFTS OF THE SPIRIT

This chapter is near to my heart because it is about the Holy Spirit and His Gifts. The Pentecostal church is mentioned quite a few times in this chapter because it was in this church that I was introduced to the Holy Spirit. I was indoctrinated to their way of believing having to do with the baptism in the Holy Spirit and speaking in tongues. I hope they understand I am not pointing a finger at them with some things I say. My concern is about a doctrine they teach that I believe is not completely correct according to God's word. My understanding of God's word is different then how they teach their doctrine. I have been exposed to this doctrine for seventy plus years and been bothered by it until I believe God has showed me why. This is why I am sharing what I believe is the truth.

The first part of this chapter is about me and my family and why I'm writing about this very important subject. The second part explains what I believe is scriptural proof that their teaching about Salvation followed by seeking the Baptism in the Holy Spirit is not only based on a wrong interpretation of scripture, but, is also based on what happened in 1906 in San Francisco and I believe is somewhat flawed.

MY CHRISTIAN EXPERIENCES AND CONCERNS ABOUT THE CHURCH.

My family and I attended a Pentecostal church for many years and stopped going for many reasons. I attended Pentecostal churches all my life. One of the main reasons for dropping out of church was because of the secular political system some people were bringing in to control the body of Christ and this is still going on.

In 1997 my family and I started attending a Pentecostal church again after not attending church for a few years. The reason for attending this church is mainly because I was raised under the Pentecostal doctrine. My wife and I raised our children under the same doctrine. I understand where the Pentecostal church originated and what I have to say will not make some Pentecostals happy. God was speaking to my heart in a very clear way. He was asking me to teach and write about His word, especially about Baptism and His gifts. I started my study on baptism and the gifts and presented my findings to several ministers and many laymen in this Pentecostal church I was attending. Just recently I've shared with Christians from other denominations and receive a very good response. Before getting into what I believe God has showed me about His Gifts and baptism, I would like to share with you what God has done in my life.

During my youth I was quite an introvert about doing certain things in church, and was always intimidated by Bible scholars or people I now describe as church politicians. Who was I to question or disagree with the Elders of the church about a Doctrine we were instructed to live our daily lives by. I was taught to honor the church leaders so I looked up to them as being closer to God because of their walk and responsibilities. As time passed I learned that these leaders were not as holy as I thought. Some of these people were Holier then Thou while in church, but holy terrors out of church. This caused me to start taking a serious look at the church and who these leaders were. My wife and I had and still have a difficult time with the politics being played, so for this reason for periods of time my family and I did not attend church. While attending this church I did earn and receive an Associates Degree in Bible Theology.

I believe satan has deflected the real truth about God's word and man fell for it. This caused some Christians to not join in with the Pentecostal movement over the years. I believe this caused the Christian church (body of Christ) to be fractured and stay this way, no unity. I am only sharing with everyone what God is showing me after seventy years of exposure to a battle between Christian churches. This is being done through a thorough study of his word without signing on to any particular denominational doctrine. I believe the church (body of Christ) has gone far enough on mans ideas. It's time to open our eyes and ask God for His Holy Spirit to deal with this problem by showing all born again Christians the truth about how man has taken control and left Him out.

I was exposed to what Pentecostals taught about the Baptism in the Holy Spirit, and especially their interpretation of the gifts of tongues, interpretation of, and prophecy. At a young age I read my Bible but didn't understand all I was reading, so I listened to elders, pastors, evangelist, and Sunday school teachers, and out of respect trusted them. I had limited understanding of God's word having to do with the baptism and the gifts at that time. When I got older I started studying more and now I would like to share with you how I understand why God made these gifts available to New Testament Christians which include us today. All Pentecostal churches that I attended while I was growing up taught salvation first and followed by seeking the Baptism in the Holy Spirit which included speaking in tongues as the evidence, and this gave Christians God's power. This meant if you didn't speak in tongues you were not Baptized in the Holy Spirit. Because of the way I was taught, I always wondered myself whether speaking in tongues was the only evidence. I couldn't find this in the scriptures. The way this was pushed on people was of great concern to me. I do believe in tongues (languages) and interpretation because it is in God's word, but not the way it was being taught to me and others and this still continues today.

As time passed, I began gaining more insight in the word, and I didn't believe it was necessary to do what they were doing. I could not find it anywhere in the scriptures. This type of nonsense didn't occur on the Day of Pentecost. The disciples believed, began speaking, and through the Holy Spirit, words came out in another language. This is the supernatural occurrence the Bible speaks of. They did not ask for it, God gave it to them as one of the gifts through His Holy Spirit. Can you imagine, nobody knew what was about to take place. It was a surprise to all, not only to the disciples, but everyone there. This same supernatural occurrence happened in the town of Joppa (Acts 11:15-16) where it says, (15) "when I began to speak, the Holy Spirit fell on them just as He did on us in the beginning [Acts 2:1-4]. Then I recall what the Lord said, John indeed baptized with water, but ye shall be baptized with (be placed in, introduced to) the Holy Spirit."

After doing a thorough study on the gifts and with the Holy Spirit, I will say this with confidence. I believe the Holy Spirit enters us at rebirth, after repentance, and receiving Christ as our Savior. We should then study and seek the truth for our understanding. As we grow and become mature in His word the Holy Spirit will do His part by filling us with God's love to overflowing, giving us His power to do as His Son Jesus and the disciples did, and perform many wonders. This would include the nine gifts. We would receive the gifts as His Holy Spirit willed them. Languages would be a part of this, speaking and praising God in a heavenly language (only known to God), not for interpretation, speaking in other languages (known to man), and interpreting when necessary. This would all be done in a manner which would represent the Father to the world without embarrassment and done orderly through the Holy Spirit.

No where in scripture does it say speaking in tongues is the evidence of the baptism in the Holy Spirit. As Christians we should not base a doctrine on just a few scriptures. All scriptures should be put into context so the truth can be brought out. Tongues (languages) is a gift for the Christians to use when the Holy Spirit wills it necessary, and tongues (languages) are not to be used to confuse, but to uplift the Body of Christ. The Holy Spirit willed it necessary at the day of Pentecost for a good reason. It was to show God's supernatural power to the unbelieving Jews and Gentiles at that time. These were known languages understood by the people in the crowd, not the ones speaking. I was always embarrassed when trying to explain the Pentecostal way of teaching about this. Discussing this with secular people or other Christians that didn't believe it and I couldn't prove it by His word. Just recently I had a discussion with two Pentecostal ministers and I ask them if they could defend their doctrine about the baptism with the Holy Spirit and speaking in tongues, and their answer was, they could not. I had the same discussion with the entire leadership of another church which included three ministers and two elders and they said it wasn't necessary to speak in tongues to be baptized with the Holy Spirit. This was a complete change in their teaching about a doctrine they had taught for years. Today, I believe they are teaching the original doctrine again. I believe this was caused by internal pressure by some in the inner circle of the leadership (politics).

What we must do when the supernatural power of God falls is to clothe ourselves with the whole armor of God because the devil will show up and attack at the same time. Christians think that when the Holy Spirit falls, everything is wonderful and there are no problems. The latter unfortunately is not always so. Christians fail to understand that satan will show up and attack at the same time. Being ignorant of that fact will cause major problems for you. For example, when the Azusa Street Revival was going strong in 1906-07, manifestations of witchcraft occurred in the same meeting. When the Holy Spirit was moving, some people moved out in the flesh. That's one of the reasons why the Azusa Street Revival ended before its' time. I believe during this revival satan slithered his way in again and deceived some people.

I understand how some Christians would feel when hearing about or being in a Pentecostal meeting. I observed people in many church meetings when nothing but their flesh was in control and the minister and elders let it happen, saying nothing. God showed me how hypocritical this was. I have never seen a minister defend Gods word when someone in their congregation was out of order, doing things in the flesh. The Holy Spirit moves more freely in some Pentecostal churches because of the way people worship. I don't believe all that happens in these meetings is of God because of mans flesh. Being pushed to the floor and convincing the person they are under the power of God is one example. Another is telling people they must speak in tongues to be baptized in the Spirit. There are no scriptures that say or prove that statement. Another would be telling people they are healed because God showed you they were. If those people aren't healed and they die because of what you said, you should be held accountable and stop doing that or get out of the ministry. I call this, mans control, not the Holy Spirit.

Why would the Holy Spirit (God's power) need others to help Him? The Holy Spirit is part of the Trinity and I can't find anything in the scriptures where He tries to push people to the floor. He is a gentleman and has everything under control, and if He wants you on the floor, He will place you there without any assistance from man. I remember the leadership always having sheets or blankets to cover the women if they fell (by being pushed) to the floor because they wore dresses. My belief is if it was the Holy Spirit doing it they would not need a blanket. I said he is a gentleman. I observed many women over the years when under the influence of the Holy Spirit sitting where they were without being pushed or helped to the floor. Mans idea was to get you on the floor so they could say you were being slain in the Spirit. They have fooled many people this way.

I believe Pentecostals, over the years, have taken some scriptures out of context, misinterpreted, and misused the gifts of the Spirit. All the gifts are very important to the whole church. All parts of the Body of Christ need to function, not just a few. If God wanted everyone to have the gift of speaking in tongues and interpretation, He would have said so. It is a gift of God's power and not the required evidence of being baptized, as Pentecostals believe. The evidence of being able to use the gifts is a sign of God's power through His Holy Spirit, not the evidence of only one. Any of the gifts can be evidence of His filling. In the scriptures, it says there are diversities of operation, but it is the same spirit which works all in all. It also mentions all the gifts and explains that not one will get all, but they will be divided among the Body of Christ. It appears that the Pentecostals think they have control of the church (Body of Christ), when there are many other Christians taking part.

After salvation, Pentecostals get caught up on being baptized in the Holy Spirit which I believe we already have at our time of regeneration. The reason why they had to wait is because Jesus was still here. His assignment was not yet completed. The Holy Spirit could not begin His work (baptizing people into Jesus Christ) until Jesus returned to the Father. In John 16:7 (KJV), it says, "Nevertheless I tell you the truth; it is expedient for you that I go away: for if I go not away, the Comforter will not come unto you; but if I do depart, I will send Him unto you".

When Jesus was in the Upper Room with the disciples, (John20:22 KJV) He said, "I breathe on you, receive ye the Holy Spirit". Jesus meant what He said and they received the Holy Spirit immediately. Even though they received the Holy Spirit they could not use His power until the Day of Pentecost. This is the day they were all filled with God's Spirit. Christians today do not have to wait because the Holy Spirit is available instantly upon regeneration and this is the evidence of receiving the baptism in the Holy Spirit. All Christians have to do at this point is study His word, follow in His footsteps, obey His commands, accept His Gifts, and He will fill you to overflowing with His Spirit.

For many years, I was under the impression that Acts 2:13 (KJV)meant the disciples were seen staggering as though they were drunk with wine. This is what was taught in the church. I suppose the thought was, they were filled with wine, and the wine had control of them. They were filled, but not with wine, but with the Holy Spirit and He had control. It was like being filled to overflowing with the Spirit of God, and I believe this does happen. After some study I have concluded the scriptures are relating to the disciples speaking in other languages and not staggering as they walked. They were talking like people who had been drinking wine. Most people under the influence of much alcohol will slur their speech. So when the people heard them speaking, they thought they had been drinking wine, but what they were really doing was drinking in God's Spirit and speaking in other languages they did not know, but other ethnic groups understood them. This was done by God's supernatural power.

Let me share one of my supernatural encounters I had with God. I was worshipping God in church with no one touching me and the Holy Spirit came upon me as like beads of oil flowing down my face, arms, and body. At first, it alarmed me and I didn't want to open my eyes for a period of time. I was afraid to share this with anyone at the time it happened. I thought they would think I was making it up. This is what satan wanted me to do, keep quiet. I eventually shared this happening with another Christian. I was convinced the Holy Spirit was anointing me with God's love and they agreed. When reflecting back on this experience, I know what God was showing me. There are signs that follow His infilling and His Spirit will do this without all the outward show of the flesh. I do believe the Holy Spirit can do anything, any way He wants, but I also believe when He does it everything will be done according to the scripture and in order. I believe that was God's anointing on my life. The timing on when and what to do with this anointing was some concern to me, but entirely up to God. I was happily married with three children and a very good job. Many doors opened for me, not only in church but at my job. I don't want to take time now to share all that happened, but I will in another book. God is good!!

I truly believe God had given me the gift of discernment and I did not know how to deal with it until I really started studying His word and praying for God to open my eyes to the truth. Some of my time spent while not going to church, was not being a very good Christian, but the Holy Spirits conviction on my life was constantly there. I was always thinking about my walk with God and how I was taught certain things about His word. I started studying, praying, and trying to understand why all other churches didn't believe in the Pentecostal experience today. That is what I was taught, Pentecostals were right, the other churches were wrong. God has shown me many things that are wrong in God's church and I will share some in this chapter.

Here is another supernatural encounter I had with God. This happens when you talk with Him and ask questions. As I've said to others, God might not talk to you in an audible voice, but if you listen, He will communicate with you in many different ways. On March 15, 2001, at 4:30am, I was awakened from my sleep rather abruptly, like a shock and I was not dreaming or having a nightmare. God projected before my eyes a message. The message told me to continue reading His word about His Holy Spirit and the spiritual gifts and He would continue to show me the truth. I am doing this now and will continue because I know He will keep revealing truths to me. God knows my heart, so I have asked Him to show me through His Holy Spirit whether certain things happening in churches are true to scripture, in order, and not of the flesh.

I ask you to read what God has given me to share. I know some of what you will read is not what has been taught you, but I ask you to be patient until you have finished reading and prayed about it, giving God the last word. I remember a testimony given by a Doctor some years ago who specialized in eye surgery. He was Catholic and his testimony had to do with the Catholic Church, and what he was taught by the Priest during his youth. Not remembering his entire testimony, I do remember him saying he was somewhat confused about what the Priest had taught him comparing that to what he eventually read for himself in the Bible. His conclusion was if you ask God to reveal His word to you He will do so. What was taught him did not match what he read in Gods word. I believe this has always been the Catholic Church problem. Reading the Bible is a must for everyone, not just the a few. Man has the right to read and understand what God's word says, not having someone telling him what it says and means. We are not living back during the Inquisitions when you would be put to death for reading the Bible.

It is like giving a book report in school without reading the book. We would all fail if we did that. We all fail the Holy Spirit (our teacher), if we don't read and understand what His word says and means for ourselves. If we really believe in God and satan, we can't expect the Minister or Priest to stand in for us when ask a question that is critical to our salvation. You can't say to satan, the Minister or Priest has my answer. We have to stand before God, one on one, on the Day of Judgment.

The Lord promised to send a comforter who would join us to Him and He did. Compare this union to a lump of dough without water. The dough cannot possess unity without the water. Likewise, all Christians, and there are many, cannot be made one in Christ without the water from heaven. The earth does not become alive unless it receives moisture from heaven to bring forth life. Jesus receiving this gift on the day of His baptism from His Father, does Himself also confer it upon those who are partakers of Himself sending the Holy Spirit upon all the earth. That happened when Jesus returned back to the Father and the Holy Spirit is still with us today. I believe man has forgotten this and he has taken control of the church.

THE TRUTH ACCORDING TO SCRIPTURE

The scriptures say the Holy Spirit's personality compared to the Father and Son, are equal. The following is a paraphrase of what it says in Unger's Bible Dictionary about the Holy Spirit. The Spirit strives with man to instruct, regenerate, sanctify, and comfort. The Holy Spirit is called God and the names given Him that properly belong to God. He has been given divine attributes, such as, knowledge and eternity. Creation and the new birth are attributed to him. Worship and homage are paid through the Holy Spirit. The sin against the Holy Spirit is the unpardonable sin. He is equal in power and glory with the Father and Son. He is sent by them, and they operate through Him and He is the source of life. The Holy Spirit took an important role in the coming of Christ and the qualifying of His human nature. For His work He is the revealer of all divine truth. The scriptures are the product of the Holy Spirit. He moves upon the hearts and consciences of all men.

A slow decline of the Pentecostal experience was seen during different periods of church history. In A.D. 30, Luke says, "That they were all filled with the Holy Ghost, and began to speak in other languages, as the Spirit gave them utterance". Again in A.D. 56, Paul wrote all about the gifts, including other languages. In the next 150 years some were still being using the prophetic gifts. By A.D. 200, the Holy Spirit and the gifts were slowly in decline in the church. By the Fourth Century it was written about the gifts of the Spirit as described in I Cor.12-14 (KJV) saying they were exceedingly obscured (vague). When reading about this, it appeared like the church wanted to discontinue using the gifts of the spirit altogether. I read about another testimony saying the gifts showed up during the middle centuries but didn't last. After many centuries, probably at the end of the 19TH or early 20TH century they say the Holy Spirit and His gifts showed up in a small church in San Francisco, California. There is a book written about how it started and how it has grown over the years to become the Pentecostal church of today.

I do believe God's gifts are for our use today, but my understanding about how they should be used is different from some Pentecostals and other denominations. I'll try to explain when and where it all started and how they have been and still are used by the Pentecostal church for over one hundred years, and you'll want to dive into you're

Bible and investigate. If you read this from an intellectual standpoint only and not include the spiritual standpoint it will not resonate with you. Some will say I'm crazy and will completely disagree with what I say, especially those who have been caught up in what I believe God has showed me are misinterpretations of the scriptures (mans intellectual interpretation). This has been going on for years and when your eyes are opened to the truth it will be very embarrassing. When I write about this subject it reminds me of how the Catholic Church first started worshiping the mother Mary. I believe it happened in the 12th century when other religious groups (idol worship) were competing with them. Their primary rivals were Iris of Egypt, Ishtar of Babylon, and Athena of Greece. So, they made this change by adding mother Mary to their worship and she has been there ever sense. I believe some Catholic Churches around the world still worship her instead of Jesus. Another one of mans way of taking control.

Spiritual gifts were given to all Christians in New Testament times by God. The day Jesus was baptized by John the Baptist, and the Holy Spirit came down from Heaven, and settled upon Him, was the day the power of God was given to be used by Christians with His guidance. In Acts 10:37-38 (KJV) it says, "that [same] message which was proclaimed throughout all Judea, starting with Galilee after the baptism preached by John, how God anointed and consecrated Jesus of Nazareth with the [Holy] Spirit and with strength and ability and power; how He went about doing good and, in particular, curing all who were harassed and oppressed by the [the power of] the devil, for God was with Him". By

Jesus using the power of the Holy Spirit, started what the Father asked Him to do and when Jesus reached a point in His ministry when it was coming to an end, He prepared the disciples to continue His ministry, first by His authority and then by guidance and power of the Holy Spirit.

In Acts 19:2-6 (Amplified Bible), it says (2) "And he asked them, did you receive the Holy Spirit when you believed [on Jesus as the Christ]? And they said, no, we have not ever heard that there is a Holy Spirit. (3) And he asked, into what [baptism] then were you baptized? They said, into John's baptism. (4) And Paul said John baptized with the baptism of repentance, continually telling the people that they should believe in the one who was to come after them, that is, in Jesus [having a conviction full of joyful trust that He is Christ, the Messiah, and being obedient to Him]. (5) On hearing this, they were baptized [again], this time in the name of the Lord Jesus. (6) And as Paul laid his hands upon them, the Holy Spirit came on them; and they spoke in [foreign, unknown] tongues (languages) and prophesied." The tongues (foreign, unknown) were unknown to the speaker, if to the listener it would have mentioned the necessity for interpretation.

Compare these scriptures. In John 20:19-22 (KJV), "When Jesus appeared in the locked room with eleven of the twelve disciples". His appearance was to provide confirmation of His resurrection and by doing this, they believed and He instilled in them His Holy Spirit by breathing on them. In Genesis 2:7 (KJV) it says, "And the Lord God formed a man of the dust of the ground, and breathed into his nostrils the breath of life, and man became a living soul". The breathing

187

of Jesus on the disciples was a rebirth (born again), and then "Receive ye the Holy Ghost". The gift of the Spirit is Christ's re-creation. He gave His own breath and Spirit. In this hour, because the disciples' believed His death and resurrection, they received re-birth. The breathing of Jesus on the disciples compares to Adam's creation. This same thing happens to us at salvation.

After receiving the Holy Ghost, Jesus tells them not to begin telling others yet, stay here in the city until the Holy Spirit comes and fills you with power from Heaven. The Holy Spirit could not come with power until Jesus returned to the Father. The disciples could not receive the power until this happened. Today, we don't have to wait, Jesus is at the right hand of the Father and the Holy Spirit is immediately with us with His power. Prior to John the Baptist baptizing Jesus, He did not have the power to use the gifts. After His baptism by the Holy Spirit He performed many wonders. This same supernatural happening occurred on the Day of Pentecost. In Jesus' case during Johns baptism of Him, the heavens opened and the Spirit of God came upon Him as like a dove, this was God's power. This same supernatural occurrence happened to the disciples in the upper room, the Holy Spirit came like a mighty wind and what looked like tongues of fire came upon them, this was God's power. Jesus waited thirty years for this power, the disciples only waited forty days.

After the Holy Spirit had baptized them, meaning purifying them in the upper room, He then filled them with His power on the day of Pentecost. They could then use the gifts through the Holy Spirit and His guidance to show great effects. One of these great effects was speaking in other languages. This is the supernatural utterance through their voice. The disciples did not know what God was preparing them to do. God spoke through them in other languages they did not know. Paul regarded tongues (languages) as a "sign" to unbelievers (I Cor.14:22), and in that context it appears like he means un-interpreted tongues, such as occurred at Pentecost. Tongues (languages) that were interpreted were for the edification of the church. This would be God's supernatural way of giving someone the understanding of any language spoken even though the speaker did not know the language.

The use of the word tongues in scripture means the same as languages, so I will continue to use languages in place of tongues. The disciples could then speak in other languages without the need for interpretation, prophesying, and many other wonders like Christ performed. The disciples believed and received the Holy Spirit. They were then told to wait until the Spirit filled them. God's Spirit could then start His work, baptizing people into Christ.

I like what it says in scripture about John the Baptist, "For He shall be great in the sight of the Lord, and shall drink neither wine nor strong drink, and he shall be filled with the Holy Ghost, even from the mother's womb". God's Spirit was in him from birth. It also says about the disciples, "And when they had prayed, the place was shaken where they were assembled together, and they were all filled with the Holy Ghost, and they spoke the word of God with boldness". This filling of God's Spirit was the same as Jesus received

SAMUEL D. SCULL

and He and the disciples received God's power to do great wonders.

The revelation of the gospel to the world did not come to men through the apostles speaking in other languages on the Day of Pentecost. It came through the preaching of the gospel in a language known to the speaker and understood by the people. The church soon learned that outsiders were afraid and confused when a person spoke in other languages. In the 1st Century, Paul had to tell believers that in public places languages must be spoken in order and according to the scripture. Paul is the one who said, "I thank God I speak with languages more than you all in private, yet in the church I had rather speak five words with my understanding than by my voice, that I might teach others also, than ten thousand words in an unknown language" (unknown to the people he was addressing). It makes no difference whether it is a heavenly language or different ethnic languages it's still confusing to the people if they don't understand them. All of God's gifts are of a supernatural nature and will not confuse the people. If it's confusing, it's not from God.

Paul wrote, "If therefore the whole church come together into one place, and all speak with languages" as an indication that all the early Christians did indeed speak with other languages. Paul said, "I would that ye all speak with other languages", meaning, he wished they all spoke with other languages, but they didn't. I agree with what Paul said, it's the word of God and it's the truth. Just remember, he said the church, meaning all believers, not unbelievers. I believe today God's people can worship Him in a (heavenly language) if it's not confusing and done while non-Christians

190

are not present. It would be absolutely confusing and would frighten sinners into not wanting anything to do with it. I have friends this happened to some years ago and they still will not go to church and especially a Pentecostal church today.

If its languages like on the Day of Pentecost I would agree that the gift should be used with sinners present. The gift would show the sinner how God can use His power through His Holy Spirit to guide an individual in speaking in another language, and interpret if necessary. This was the great effect He showed through the disciples, using His power. If I was there, it surely would have convinced me of His power. If this was happening today, it would also convince me and many others the flesh has disappeared and the Holy Spirit is here with His supernatural power. If the heavenly language is being used with an interpretation, I believe it not according to scripture. Heavenly language is between you and God via the Holy Spirit and is private.

You decide to accept Jesus Christ as your savior and you can decide how you want to live your Christian life. God gave us a will to make our own decisions as He did our first parents. This is part of our development in the Holy Spirit who the Christian receives earlier by faith at salvation. Remember what it says in 1Cor.12 (KJV); "there are diversities of gifts and no one will get them all". It will not work for the body of Christ if one gets all. Read the whole chapter and especially pay attention to what it says about the body of Christ. Pentecostals have and still are living an unbalanced Christian life by only having a few people use their gifts that the Holy Spirit willed to them.

This is only an example of how our bodies are supposed to function compared to the body of Christ. The church is supposed to function like our human body. In order for our body to function properly everything must be coordinated by the brain. If this don't happen out human body will not function as it should. Our arms might not move, or our legs might not function so we won't be able to walk. You know what I mean. The brain (head) of the church body is Jesus Christ. It is through His Spirit that each part of His body gets the proper coordination (balance). If we Christians decide only a few get the gifts the church body will not function properly. In other words if we believe in the gifts and they are being used today in the church, we need to make sure the distribution is by the Holy Spirit and not man.

I remember ministers and elders saying if tongues didn't follow your baptism, you didn't receive the baptism in the Holy Spirit. The deacons or elders would pray with you to receive the baptism and if you didn't make a sound like babbling, they would coach you by telling you to start mumbling (not scriptural). If you did this, they would tell the pastor or evangelist you had stammering lips which was the same to them as speaking in tongues. Being a gullible young man I believed what my elders were saying. After all they were supposed to know more about God's word than me. In Sunday school we listened and learned about Jesus and the great men and woman of the Bible and nothing was ever taught about the gifts and how they operate.

Some Pentecostal still use this tactic but deny it if questioned. Believe me when I say this type of thing happened in all Pentecostal meetings I ever attended, including the Pentecostal Business Men's Association of New Jersey. I remember as I was going through my teen years and considering myself being baptized in the Holy Spirit but I never spoke in tongues (another language) as everyone else claimed they had and I was always bothered by that. When I heard people speak in what I considered a strange tongue in church, the thought always occurred to me, was that person really speaking in another language according to scripture or was it how they were instructed by others how to do it and it became an emotional reaction, a human behavior? After many years thinking I was the only one this happened to, I found out I was wrong, there were others. There are those who have written, saying tongues (speaking in another language) is not the evidence of being baptized in the Holy Spirit. There are others who agree, but afraid to express themselves. There also are those who will agree, but when put to the test reverse their agreement for political reasons.

People that went through this experience say they were filled with the Holy Spirit and yet some continue to be disagreeable, emotionally unstable, and difficult to communicate with. They have to be kidding themselves. Such behavior is not caused by the Holy Spirit. Others who claim to have had this type experience with the Holy Spirit negate their claim by continuing to manifest the works of the flesh, such as anger, jealousy, and worry. They fail to see that the Holy Spirit wants to change their emotions. Pentecostals say this experience gives you Gods power. Where is it? Where is their church any different than other mainline churches?

This kind of attitude is keeping church unity in a box and not allowing it to grow together for His coming.

People truly filled with the Holy Spirit will show it by their behavior. The best way I know to clarify the term spirit-filled is to point out the real meaning, "control". In Eph. 5:18 (KJV), it is compared negatively to someone who is controlled by alcohol. "Do not be drunk with wine, in which is in excess, but be filled with the Spirit". It is the most powerful command in the Bible to be "filled or controlled by the Holy Spirit". Look again at the context. A drunken person is filled with wine when controlled by the substance. The person isn't literally filled with a liquid, but if the substance controls him, it will alter his behavior, mentally, emotionally, and physically.

Political, meaning they would rather compromise God's truth than have a debate on whether it's true or not. Being afraid of what others would say or think is not being a strong Christian. Continuing to believe others are wrong in their teaching and not standing up to defend God's word makes you a hypocrite. There are still a few Christians in God's church who don't follow this line of thinking that tongues are the only evidence. They still have the check and balance the word talks about. In I Cor.14:29 (KJV), it says, "Let the prophets speak two or three, and let the others judge". Not everything said in church is true and according to God's word, and Christians need to know the truth. Praying that God would allow the church to use the gifts of wisdom and knowledge would be a good start.

All ministers according to God's word are called by Him, not by man. In most churches today it doesn't work that way. I don't have a problem with people going to Christian colleges for learning. I do have a problem with people using their Christian education to get a position as a pastor and they were not really called by God to be in that position. I believe this is one of the reasons why the church has fallen apart today. There are too many ministers not called by God trying to fill the pastor position and others that I call crooks, steeling the church blind and just using the position for job security. Other office holders are appointed by the minister or elected by the people. If this is not done properly man gets involved and this is where secular politics enters the church and things go down hill. All leaders are to meet the qualifications according to God's word. I don't believe in political means to gain a position in a church. I always understood that God would fill these positions, not by political means, but by spiritual means, through prayer. Man has forgotten that God sent His Holy Spirit to guide and comfort us after his Son's ascension. It is through God's word that people are chosen to fulfill certain positions in the church.

SPIRITUAL GIFTS

Spiritual gifts have always been, as indicated in the Old Testament. All but two gifts listed in the New Testament which included the word of wisdom, knowledge, faith, healing, miracles, prophecy, discerning of spirits, interpretation, were active during Old Testament times. The gift of tongues (other languages) and interpretation was added in the New Testament at the Day of Pentecost. The gift of language interpretation was not used at the Day of Pentecost, because it was not necessary. They spoke in languages that were understood by the diverse ethnic makeup of the crowd. Interpretation of these languages was not mentioned until Paul spoke about spiritual gifts in I Cor.12. There are no illustrations of it being used in scripture. It is not God's power that has changed from dispensation to dispensation, but the incidence of that power and the manner of His communication. He is the same now as He was in the Old Testament.

There are some gifts of the Spirit that became new at the Day of Pentecost, but the power behind them was always there. On the Day of Pentecost, the Holy Spirit came down from Heaven to earth and entered the body and mind of the redeemed. Today He operates in our hearts using us to show "great effects" in a supernatural way as He did with the disciples. In the Old Testament God ministered to men by the Holy Ghost from Heaven. Since Pentecost, the Holy Spirit works directly with man because He is dwelling in him. He was with us before Pentecost and now He is with us after Pentecost. In the Old Testament men experienced divine power, in the New Testament they received divine power. The Holy Ghost descended upon man in the Old Testament, in the New Testament He fills them. In the Old Testament God used certain individuals to speak for Him, in the New Testament He uses all Christians to speak for Him. A spiritual gift is the supernatural way God gives Christians to do things greater then His Son did. They operate for the furtherance of the welfare of the church through the power of the Holy Spirit.

Spiritual gifts that God gave us to use are of a supernatural nature. Christians need to believe in supernatural occurrences from God because they are scriptural. What happened to our faith and all things are possible to him who believes? Remember the old saying from our childhood "don't do as I do, do as I say?" Christians say the same thing. Some teach God's word to others but do the opposite in their daily walk. Did Jesus do this? If He were here on earth today, He would probably remove most church leaders. If people say He wouldn't because this is not showing love, I would disagree. I would say His love is shown by not allowing Christians to continue in the sin of hypocrisy. As long as man continues his human behavior, doing the things talked about here, the church will continue to fail most of the time because of man's flesh and not God's Spirit. Some will say I'm crazy just look at how the Christian movement has expanded around the world. Many souls are being saved every day. I would say God doesn't want some souls He wants them all. There is and always has been a war for mans soul and this war is going to get worse. The enemy is hard at work and the average Christian and secular people don't quite understand this is not a typical war of economics, politics, science and culture, but a war between Heaven and Hell. The war is between God and Lucifer, the deceiver, and guess who it's being waged over, mans souls.

Christians need to take God's word more serious when it comes to interpretation. It's difficult for me to understand why Christians of all denominations have never been able to iron out their differences. The word says we become one in Christ and the body of Christ is supposed to be in unity, but I believe it is not. Each denomination wants to go their way making the body of Christ unstable and not trusted. This means only one thing to me, man is in control and not the Holy Spirit. Man decides how Christians should believe and not God. Christians need to step up to the plate and as the saying goes, grab the bull by the horns, stand their ground, but do it according to God's word, not mans.

God is showing some that the church has drifted away from His truth. It's like looking into a mirror at oneself and seeing someone else, someone you would like to be. Some Ministers are teaching what the people want to hear and not what God wants them to hear. This all leads to why some Christian interpretation having to do with the gifts and how they should operate is out of order. It all has to do with human behavior. Man wants to believe in God as long as he can control what God says. Man forgets that God wrote the word and we can't add to or take away from what he says. This is why I use the King James Bible for my studies and not a version that has been changed by man to suit his beliefs. I do use the Amplified Bible for some added emphasis once in awhile.

Salvation is a gift and the most important gift. This decision we all should make during our life time here on this earth is the most important. This decision determines whether we spend eternity in Heaven or Hell. If you're reading this for the first time and you are having thoughts of whether to believe what the Bible says or you're questioning the whole Christian way of life, please take time, don't wait, we must believe that God will do as He says. You don't want to miss the bus. Don't look at what mistakes man has made, just chose the right road and be on the winner's side. While spending time on earth Christians must understand that our Father in Heaven gave us some commands and standards to follow. Those commands and standards are necessary for us to live a pure and obedient life, which is what God has always wanted for us. From the time of mans creation God has wanted him to obey. He gave one command to Adam and Eve with freedom and dominion over the earth. They were in charge but could not fulfill the one command.

He gave us a free will to decide for ourselves whether we would or wouldn't adhere to His standards. He only gave our first parents one command. In Genesis 2:16-17 (KJV) it says, "And the Lord God commanded the man, saying, of every tree of the garden thou mayest freely eat: But of the tree of the knowledge of good and evil, thou shalt not eat of it: for in the day that thou eatest thereof thou shalt surely die. Adam and Eve would have lived forever if they didn't disobey God. Satan fed Eve some lies and she thought she could fool God by changing what He said. Satan made a mistake by thinking he could be above God and was thrown out of Heaven. Did Eve have similar thoughts about being a god? Satan is the author of lies and our first parents fell for it. Do we have to? No!!! Just think if our first parents had obeyed God's only command to them we would not have needed the Ten Commandments and His Son Jesus would not have suffered on the cross. We all would be living in an expanded Garden forever.

SAMUEL D. SCULL

In II John (KJV), verse 6, it says, "Christian love demands that we walk in the truth, and that we not turn a blind eye to error." After studying God's word and things written by other Christian authors concerning the subject of spiritual gifts, it has been a confirmation in what God is showing me about concerns I have with some interpretations of His word. The spiritual gifts mention in 1Corinthians 12 are very important to a Christian in their daily walk with the Lord. These gifts were and still are given to all who accept Jesus Christ as their savior. These gifts were also available in the Old Testament times to certain individuals. These gifts will be explained in more detail in a chapter to follow. These gifts are available for our use today through the guidance of the Holy Spirit. My prayer is, please pray, read, and study all I am saying before coming to a conclusion. Ask God for His guidance.

HUMAN BEHAVIOR

I would like to share a few things about human behavior and how it affects the church. When God created man he gave him dominion over the earth and everything in it. They didn't know right from wrong at that time. They only knew what God freely gave them and what He commanded them not to do. There was only one command, and that was to not eat of the fruit of one specific tree. They knew God and all He wanted was for them to be obedient. Because Eve listened to satan and trusted what he said, man's conscience was born. God gave man a free will and he decided to be disobedient knowing what the consequence would be. So God needed to show man even though He loved them, it was necessary they know right from wrong. Even though they disobeyed Him, He still loved them, but they needed to know who their enemy was. The war began with our spirit, between good and evil.

Because of what happened with our first parents the human behavior has followed these same guide lines. Man continues to know that things will happen when doing something right or wrong. It becomes either positive or negative reinforcement to what we do. Clinical Psychologists developed the following about human behavior. They are the ABC's of human behavior. As children, we learn these ABC's very quickly. A= "antecedent" this comes before a behavior and warns us what will happen if we do it. God did that same thing and the antecedent was His one command to Adam and Eve, don't eat of a certain tree or you will die (spiritually). B= "behavior" this comes after the antecedent and shows what the person dose. Adam and Eve's behavior came after God's command. They didn't follow God's command leading to a consequence. C= "consequence" this comes after the behavior and determines whether the behavior was right or wrong. Our first parents knew what the consequence was because of their behavior.

One of the first things children learn from most parents is about right and wrong. Example: The antecedent here is "don't do that or I'll smack your hand, or in our society today, they set them in a chair in the corner, or take their TV privilege away for a couple of hours". In Adam and Eve's case the antecedent was "not to eat of the one tree or they would surely die". These antecedents came before the behavior. The knowledge of knowing if you do certain things you will be punished. We have a choice, don't do it or do it. The choice we make is our behavior, right or wrong. According to what choice we make will determine the consequence. In the child's case its punishment, and in Adam and Eve's case it was punishment which was spiritual death. If you follow this logic, you can match it with many things that God did throughout the Bible and this continues to be used in our society today. Our lives are based on the ABC's and will determine where we will end up, Heaven or Hell.

We live our lives around the ABC's in the world and in church. Where some Christians get into trouble is there is a difference between our human behavior and our spiritual behavior. We have a problem getting them both in line with each other. We think we can turn it on and off anytime we want. During the week we live according to the human (flesh) behavior, and on Sundays we try to turn our spiritual behavior on. God calls this hypocrisy in His word. Who is controlling who? Our human (flesh) behavior should be controlled by the new man in us because of what Jesus Christ did. If our human (flesh) behavior is in tune with our spiritual behavior daily, there is no hypocrisy and this is what we should be striving for. The problem is we humans are stalled in a quagmire and can't seem to get out. Why? In Eph. 6:12 it says, "For we wrestle not against flesh and blood, but against principalities, against powers, against rulers of the darkness of this world, against spiritual wickedness in high places". So, if we are Christians and understand who we are in battle with, why are we allowing our human (flesh) behavior to control what we do? I remember one of my encounters with God in a small Pentecostal church when I was twenty five years of age. It was during the worship part of the service while I was worshipping in my quiet way. I believe in having hands laid on you according to the word, but I never liked having a minister or anyone put their hands on my head, begin shaking, praying, and try to push me to the floor. This happened every time I was prayed for. If you allowed this type of conduct and fall to the floor they would then say you were under the power of the Holy Spirit. This is a lie because it's man's power that put you there and this is not scriptural.

If we really want unity in the body of Christ, we need to stop this balancing act by joining our spiritual behavior with our human (flesh) behavior and follow in the footsteps of Jesus Christ. We need to read and study God's word daily, not just on Sundays. Our responsibility is to change our human behavior to imitate Jesus more and man less. God's church needs to operate more like the scriptures say, spiritually, not humanly. This is a difficult task but it has to be done. Man needs to get out of the way and allow the Holy Spirit to take control. Everything done in the church should have a check and balance that God requires. This would eliminate wrong happenings in the church. Everyone needs to be held responsible for their actions in the body of Christ.

A FORMULA FOR RECEIVING GOD'S BAPTISM AND HIS GIFTS:

1. Salvation first, meaning, believing in God, repenting of your sins, and receiving Christ as your savior. Regeneration happens by the cleansing of ones body

and spirit by the Holy Spirit. (Spiritual baptism). A new man (body and spirit) will appear. This is not the time for the gift of speaking in tongues. This is the time for being born again, sharing your testimony, learning about God's word and how to share the Gospel. If and when God wants you to speak in another language (tongues) He will make this happen. The Gifts are available and controlled by the Holy Spirit, not man.

2. God's Holy Spirit will enter and connect with your spirit. The power of God is there at that time. You become His temple. Because of your belief and what you have done will change your demeanor. People will see the change in you. This is God's supernatural miracle by changing your character and renewing your spirit (a new man).

3. God's Gifts become available immediately for your use at the Holy Spirits will, not yours. Study to show yourself approved. A baby in Christ must become mature in His word. As you grow from a baby Christian to a mature Christian the Holy Spirit will help guide you and give you the gift or gifts necessary for your ministry.

4. Being obedient and following the commands of Jesus will help move you closer to utilizing the Gifts. There are many gifts available to be utilized by the church and the Holy Spirit is the overseer of who receives which gift or gifts. They are all important to the development of the body of Christ. Everyone should know which gift they have been given and

how to use it. You may be given more than one, but not all.

5. Just remember, God through His Spirit is the one who gives the gifts, not man. Last but not least, this is not a game and God does not play church. When dealing with the Holy Spirit we must be serious. God is a loving God, but also serious.

CHAPTER FIFTEEN

BAPTISM

There is much to be said about baptism and how important it is to God. I believe there are two types of baptisms, one by water and the other by the Holy Spirit. Water baptism was important in the Old Testament and Holy Spirit baptism is very important in the New Testament and still is today.

When reading some Bible Commentaries and dictionaries, including the Greek on the definition of baptism, I get somewhat confused. Remember God wrote the Bible so everyone could understand it. I sometimes think intellectuals write things to confuse people for many reasons. Without going into all the detailed definitions, I would like to be as plain as I can. Baptism was used many times in the Old Testament. When ever they used water it was to cleanse everything. Water was a cleansing agent and still is today. John the Baptist used it for baptizing people unto repentance for their sins, water was the cleansing agent. Water was used until John said Jesus would baptize everyone in the Holy

Spirit and fire. I understand this remark to mean water was no longer the cleansing/purifier. God's is interested in your spirit so the Holy Spirit and Fire took over the cleansing and purifying of ones heart. The Holy Spirit comes in, kicks out the bad spirit, the fire burns the chaff and that is purifying.

I would like to go into a little more detail on how I understand the difference between these two baptisms. According to the Webster and Greek Dictionaries, baptism is a dipping under, Christian baptism emersion, a symbol of washing away sin and spiritual purification. In other words, water baptism is placing you in water as a symbol of purification. In the Bible John the Baptist baptized people in the Old Testament in water as an act of repentance and purification. John's baptism was not spiritual in nature but water purifying and cleansing the human body for God when repenting. This was not a born again experience because Jesus had not died for our sins as yet. This was only a symbol of washing away our sins. The baptism by John was not Christian, but Jewish, a baptism "unto repentance". Spiritual baptism is placing you in Christ to purify, regenerate, and become the new creature. Placing the believer in Christ is the same as being born again.

John the Baptist says in Matthew 3:11 "I indeed baptize you with water unto repentance: but he that cometh after me is mightier than I, whose shoes I am not worthy to bear: he shall baptize you with the Holy Ghost and Fire". The disciples believed that Jesus Christ was their Savior. After believing they were given the Holy Spirit by Jesus in the Upper Room (John 20:22), but had to wait until He ascended to the

Father to be filled and receive His power. They received their Holy Spirit experience after His ascension at Pentecost. We receive the experience immediately upon accepting Him as our Savior. There is no waiting period for us because He is already at His Fathers side and the Holy Spirit is here and available immediately. This occurred initially in the Upper Room by Jesus who baptized believing Jews. Later He did the same for Samaritans and Gentiles. In the teaching of the Epistles, every believer is baptized by the Spirit into Christ the moment he/she is regenerated (born again).

In Acts 18:25, they were ignorant of the Christian message and the baptism of the Holy Spirit. When they heard and believed the new message of a crucified, risen, and ascended Savior, they received the Holy Spirit, which included His baptizing ministry. The baptism of the Holy Spirit is placing the believer "in Christ". In Acts 19:1-3 "they knew no baptism but John's", and in v 4, they did not receive the Holy Spirit when they believed, because they had only heard John's message, and received only John's baptism unto repentance. In v5 they were baptized in the name of the Lord Jesus and received God's power. The reason for them utilizing the gifts immediately after their salvation was God way of showing His power to everyone. He used the gift of speaking in tongues and prophesy, tongues for the believers and prophesy for the unbelievers.

I always believed receiving a spiritual gift from God was a supernatural occurrence. There are a small percentage of people who I believe have honestly received the gift of speaking in tongues (foreign language). It is one of the gifts some will get, but not all. Pentecostals teach all will get it through the baptism of the Holy Spirit. I believe they say this because the disciples received God's power on the day of Pentecost which was after they believed Jesus was the savior. Christians need to go back and re-read why they had to wait. Jesus was still here and in control, not the Holy Spirit. He had not completed His mission so He could turn it over to the Holy Spirit, so the disciples had to wait for forty days for that to happen.

CHAPTER SIXTEEN

HEALING AND MIRICLES

I should have said this at the beginning of my book where I shared my beliefs. The Bible was written for everyone to read, but was meant to be used by Christians. A sinner can read God's word but must believe, make a decision to repent of their sins, ask God to forgive them, and accept Jesus Christ as their savior. Just believing there is a God will not put you on speaking terms with Him. God's word was written for Christians and His standards are meant to be followed. Why did God stop communicating with our first parents? They couldn't even follow the only command He gave them, obedience.

If God would stop talking to them for only being disobedient for one command, why would he talk to Christians today for breaking many of His commands. I understand we are living under God's grace which means after the born again experience we should want to be obedient. Keep that in mind when asking God to do something for you. I know Jesus stands in the gap and represents us before the Father, but He is smarter then any lawyer you know, and He knows everything about you. We can't bypass His word and what it says. We still have to answer to God in the end.

Do I believe in God's healings and miracles? Yes!!!!! Are they for today? YES!!!!! I believe most Christians do, but I also believe there are skeptics. There are Christians and secular people who do not believe this will happen today and there are legitimate reasons for thinking this way. There are three distinct types of healings, one being "Spiritual" healing used by spiritualist and they believe a dead person has the power to channel to a sick person through a psychic. Another is "faith" healing which puts all trust in anything or anyone. Then "divine" healing which is based on the Lord Jesus Christ. I believe in divine healing which is between you and God and trust that what His Son did for us is true. It can be a healing with trust or a miracle by God, what ever His will. When watching some so called healing ministries on television I can understand why some are skeptics. I also have observed healing ministries over the years in local churches where people were healed and some not healed. The question is why some and not all? I'll try to explain the reasons why by using God's word. Miracles do happen and I will share some.

When I read God's word, I understand it to be sacred, true and not to be altered. In the beginning, God's creation was perfect and done according to His laws. I am talking about His creation of man in His image, not the universe. Adam and Eve were created perfect without sin. Sin is evildoing against humanity, society, oneself, and God. They only knew to do things according to God's standards. God set the standards for our human behavior. Their disobedience was a violation of those standards. This was their sin that caused mankind to be imperfect. So everyone including Adam and Eve has the sin nature. God gives everyone a way to remove their sin nature because of what His Son Jesus Christ did at the cross. Jesus took our sins upon himself. If you're a sinner and want to be forgiven, it's simple. Everyone (Jews and Gentiles) must believe in God and what He says, than ask forgiveness of their sins, and accept His Son Jesus Christ as their savior. Their sins are removed, never to be remembered again. Remember God knows everything, so if you're not serious, He will know.

His love for man after all He put up with in the Old Testament was still there or He would not have sent His Son to suffer for our sins. Jesus was not deceived by the king of cons and did not make that deadly decision our first parents made. He defeated satan and gives everyone the same opportunity if they want it. We have the same choice that Jesus had and it's up to us which way to go. Jesus is the way-maker and He made a way for me and you.

Jesus was just like you and I living a life and enjoying it. He lived in the same conditions as everyone did back then. The difference between him and us is, he was about his Father's business. He was a student of his Fathers word and spent much time learning and teaching. When Jesus was baptized He received power from His Father to do what, live a holy life sharing how His Father wants everyone to live their lives. During His ministry the healing of the sick and the raising of the dead was performed. All healings that Jesus was involved in did not always come from his power, but by the faith of the people. His word says all you need is the faith of a mustard seed and you will be healed. Healings also come from people who have been given the gift of healing because God gave it to them or by personal faith in what God has said in His word. To make this faith work obedience to God is a good start that shows Him you have faith in His word and faith that what you ask of Him will happen. Trust is another key to getting healed. We must have faith to trust God and he will do what he says. If there is any doubt at all it will not work.

Before sharing some of the scriptures about healing let me share some true stories about healings and miracles that happened to me and others.

1. Salvation is a miracle and I've seen many people come to the Lord over the years. The ones that stuck in my mind the most were those I considered to be the worst offenders of God's standards. God's word says when you ask forgiveness for your sins and accept Jesus as your savior the old sin man in you dies and you become born again, you're a new creature (man). When looking in the eyes of a person who receives salvation you can see a new person. Their human nature is completely different than before. I've seen people with different personalities having bad spirits like arrogance, belligerent attitude, selfish, jealous, mean, overbearing, you name it they had it. After repentance and accepting Jesus as their savior the new man appeared and I could not see any bad spirits when looking into their eyes. The person was transformed, the bad spirits left because they

become a temple for the Holy Spirit which means there is no room for any other spirit. The only spirit I seen was love.

2. Another miracle that I've been exposed to over the years occurred in 1954. It was called God's answer to prayer. My mother was the prayer worrier. She had dedicated seven children to the Lord when we were babies. She continued to pray that God would protect us throughout our lives. I was not living a Christian life while I was in the Navy. I was home on leave spending some time with my family and friends. My friends were also in the service and on leave. We were visiting some of the local bars one evening and when it got close to 12:00AM and they were closing we decided to go to a bar that stayed open until 2:00am. On our way we encountered someone who wanted to race. When we reached 85 mph the driver in our car decided to make a turn of about 45 degrees to another road which would take us to this next bar. We slid sideways into a concrete barrier in front of a service station which caused the car to go end over end down the highway for about 200+ feet.

For the ones who can remember what a 49/50 Ford coupe was like, you will never understand how four people survived this accident. The windows were so small an adult could not fit through them. There were two of us in the back seat and the driver and passenger in front. The four of us were thrown out of the car. When I woke up I was about twenty rows out in a corn field with the person that was in the back seat with me lying about ten feet away. I could not get a response from him so I started looking for the driver and other passenger. I found the other passenger down the highway about two electric poles away in a ditch. He was awake but couldn't move and acted like he had broken bones in his legs.

I then started looking for the driver and finely found him. The car was upside down with its top crushed clear to the seats and both doors ripped off. The driver was not in the car. I heard a noise and found him pinned under the car. A man from one of the homes nearby called for an ambulance and then came out to help me get the driver out from under the car. When the ambulance arrived they took all four of us to the local Hospital. The Hospital treated me and my friend that was on the back seat and discharged us with no serious injuries. The driver and front seat passenger was transferred to the Naval Hospital in Philadelphia, Pa., with the possibility of the driver having internal injuries and the passenger having broken legs. They were discharged the same day with no serious injuries. When people seen the car and heard the story they were amazed at how we survived the accident. I thank God for a praying mother for God's protection even though I new I was doing wrong. I believe her prayers not only protected me, but also protected the other three from bad injuries or loosing their lives.

3. This is another miracle that happened just one month before the miracle in #2. There was four of us in my car going home after an evening out drinking and dancing in a local bar. It was a fall night, chilly and a drizzle rain so I was sticking to the speed limit because of the weather. I noticed a car ahead of me had pulled off to the side of the road and just as I got close to this car the driver decided to pull out in front of me. I hit the breaks, turned left to miss the car, spinning around in a circle, went across the highway and hit an electric pole with a transformer on it. I hit the pole dead center and only cracked it. Upon impact I pushed the steering wheel through the windshield and thought I crushed my chest. When I fell out of the car I thought I was dead. The passenger in the front seat went through the windshield. The two passengers in the back seat were thrown to the front seat. The car that pulled out in front of me never stopped to help. After the police and ambulance arrived we were taken to the hospital. The back seat passengers were not injured. The passenger in the front seat had a head full of glass particles. He was treated and discharged. They x-rayed my chest and the only thing they found was a cracked collar bone. Because of the time the Hospital didn't have anyone available to cast my shoulder. They put it in a tight sling and ask me to return the next morning. When I returned the next day I met the Doctor and he had just read the x-ray. He checked my shoulder and told me it was okay and discharged me, no sling or cast. Prayer from a prayer worrier.

4. This is another story about healing. It starts with an elderly man with a diagnosis of cancer and near death. A Minister that visited people in this hospital where this man was went to his room to talk about his condition and the Lord. When the minister first went in he found the man was completely covered with a sheet. The Medical Surgeon had already operated on him and found him full of cancer and as the minister testified, he could smell the odor from the cancer out in the hallway. The man would not respond to the ministers questions or have a conversation with him. So the minister started reading scriptures from the Bible. If you knew this man you would know he was one of the worse to get along with.

He was arrogant, disagreeable, foul mouth of the worse kind, heavy smoker and more. He didn't want to hear anything about God. Anyhow the minister would go each day, get close to his ear, and read scriptures for hours. The man would not opened his eyes or respond by voice. On the fifth day while reading scriptures the minister notice a tear drop out of one of his eyes. He started crying and finally started talking to the minister. To make a long story short he started eating, they check him for cancer and he had none. He left the hospital, started going to church and giving his testimony to anyone that would listen to him. He would go to the hospital as much as he could, visit all the sick people and give his testimony. The Doctors called him their miracle man. I don't know how many times he read his Bible, but I knew he had every word underlined with pencil or ink. I believe he lived for another twenty years and when you met him you knew he was a Christian by his smile and the look in his eyes. He was the most active Christian at his age that I ever knew.

5. I believe you could call what happened to me when I was working a miracle. I was a supervisor in a chemical plant and was sprayed in the face with a mixture of hydrochloric and hydrofluoric acid. The hydrofluoric is one of the worse known acids to man. When this acid contacts your skin it starts looking for the calcium in your bones. If it is not treated immediately it can do much damage to your body. Anyhow when it contacted the skin on my face I immediately flushed my face with water, and ran to my car. I started to drive to the medical facility about a half mile away when I was stopped by a broad gauge train crossing the road and had to wait for it to move on by. While I was sitting there I finally looked in the rear view mirror at my face and it scared me. There were blisters that ranged from dime size to quarter size, and there was a small portion on the bottom of my left ear missing.

I finally reached the medical facility and explained to the medical staff what was on my face. They put me in a bed and dumped a five gallon bucket of chipped ice over my face and head and covered it with a towel. I could hear the Doctor saying to someone, the burns were pretty severe so keep putting on ice for about an hour and then he would take a look at them. I can remember praying, please Lord heal these blisters. A feeling of peace came over my body as if the Lord said relax and don't worry. After the hour was up they removed the ice and the doctor was amazed. He said to me the blisters are gone. The blisters were gone and just a few minor spots were left. Within a few days you would never know I was ever burned. I considered this not only a healing, but a miracle. Being burn with either one of these acids and not have any scaring is a miracle.

6. This miracle was shared with me about a woman that had a growth on the side of her neck. My mother was the one sharing this so I had no reason to disbelieve her. She and a group of friends were attending a Christian service in Pennsylvania. I believe Oral Roberts was the speaker. She noticed this woman with this huge growth setting behind her. As the service progressed to a point when the speaker started praying for healing a loud scream come from the woman behind my mother. It was so loud it frightened my mother. So she turned to see what was happening. The growth on her neck had disappeared. This was a miracle. I would like to point out here, The Minister never put his hands on her nor did anyone else. It was her faith and trust that God would do what he said. Why would this happen to her and not others?

I believe there is something missing besides faith and trust and that is obedience, even though I believe all three are important to God. There are other things that God wants us to do besides having faith and trust. He set standards for us to live by and we need to ask the question, are we doing that? We might be serious when asking God for forgiveness of our sins, but are we serious about living that life He expects. If we are on the fence most of the time picking and choosing what we want to do and not what God wants us to do, I believe God turns His ear the other way. Our prayers are probably a waste of time. You might think I'm wrong when I make these statements and that is okay. All I ask of you to do is read His word and what He says about lukewarm Christians.

Here are some scriptures we need to read and put into context. Matthew 21:21, "Then Jesus told them, truly, if you have faith and don't doubt you can do things like this and much more. You can even say to this Mount of Olives, move over into this ocean, and it will." Jesus said "if you have faith", and I believe we all would say we have faith. He also said "and don't doubt", and I believe this is one of the problems where we get into trouble and our prayers don't get answered. There is always that tiny thought about whether God will or won't. Did we ever ask our self this question? Is it our will that we want this to happen or is it God's will? Before we ask God for something we need to make sure we are in right standing with Him and on talking terms with Him. We need to look in the mirror and ask our selves, am I where I need to be in Christ, talking the talk and walking the walk. I'm not talking about your salvation, I'm talking about becoming a disciple and spreading the Good News about Jesus Christ, and using the Gifts that He gave us to show His supernatural wonders.

Matt.20:22 (KJV) is the key to what I'm trying to say. He is saying you ask, but ye know not what ye ask. "Are ye able to drink of the cup that I shall drink of, and to be baptized with the baptism that I am baptized with: they say unto Him, we are able". They must have been living the life expected by God or Jesus would not have said what He said in verse 23. "Ye shall indeed drink of my cup."

Prayers are important when you know what you ask or say is in God's will.

1. Disobedience: "If you don't obey you can not pray". This saying was in some of my college material and when I ask three class instructors if they agreed with the statement, they told me no. I disagreed with them because I believe it is true. They didn't want to hear me or even discuss it, and had it removed from the syllabus. I believe you can pray, but God will not answer if you are not being obedient to His word. God gives us specific instructions about salvation and if we don't obey them, is He going to

remove our sins? Are we going to become a new creature (man) in Christ?

De.1:45 (KJV); God instructed Moses "to take the people to the hill country of the Amorites, and to all their neighbors in the Arabah, in the hill country, in the low land of the South, and on the coast, the land of the Canaanites, and Lebanon, as far as the great river Euphrates. Behold I have set the land before you; go in and take possession of the land which the Lord swore to your fathers, to Abraham, to Isaac, and to Jacob, to give to them and to their descendants after them". They were afraid of the people and did not do what God told them to do. After Moses talked to them they decided to do what God instructed. But God said it was too late and if they went, they would be going without Him which would be a disaster. They were disobedient to God. He did not answer their prayer.

1Sam.14:37 (KJV); "And Saul ask counsel of God, shall I go down after the Philistines? Will you deliver them into the hand of Israel? But He did not answer him that day." Why did God not answer? It was because of the oath Saul made his army take. They would not eat until evening, but after seeing Jonathan eat the honey because he did not know about the oath, the others did eat. They ate of the animals including the blood which was a sin against God. They violated God's law by eating the blood of animals after the battle. In verse 52 it says, "There was severe war against the Philistines all the days of Saul. God never answered Saul's request. There are many more scriptures like these when it comes to disobedience, check them for yourself.

2. Secret sin: Any unrighteous thought you regard and no one knows but you and God is a secret sin. God knows everything!!! I share with people if we get rid of the outward sins the secret sins will eventually go. If we are serious when asking forgiveness, God removes them right away. But we humans believe we have to work at removing them. That is not faith in what God's word says or trust that He will help us.

Ps.66:18 (KJV). If I regard iniquity in my heart, the Lord will not hear me. In Pr. 15:29 (KJV) it says, "The Lord is far from the wicked, but He hears the prayers of the righteous".

In Pr. 28:9 (KJV) it says "He who turns away his ear from hearing the law, even his prayer is an abomination, hateful and revolting to God".

If you are hypocritical in things you do for God, they become a burden to Him. Isa.1:15 says, And when you spread forth your hands [in prayer, imploring help], I will hide my eyes from you; even though you make many prayers, I will not hear. Your hands are full of blood.

John 9:31(KJV) says, "we know that God does not listen to sinners; but if anyone is God-fearing and a worshiper of Him and does His will, He listens to him".

If you ask God under false pretence God says this in James 4:3 (KJV); "You ask and fail to receive, because you ask with wrong purpose and evil, selfish motives. Your intention is [when you get what you desire] to spend it in sensual pleasures".

3. Indifference: If you have a lack of concern about what God is saying or wanting you to do and you don't listen to His counsel, accept His reproof, means you are disregarding Him. When you really need Him and call upon Him He will not answer. Pr.1:28 (KJV); "then they will call upon Him and I will not answer; they will seek me diligently but will not find me". Other scriptures (KJV) Job 27:9; 35:12, 13; Isa.1:15,16; Jer.11:11; Mic.3:4; James 4:3.

4. Neglect of mercy: Mercy is a divine quality. God shows it in many ways such as kindness, goodness, grace, favor, pity, compassion and many more synonyms we could use. When we neglect them we neglect mercy.

Pr.21:13 (KJV); "whoever stops his ears at the cry of the poor will cry out himself and not be heard".

Matt.18:35 (KJV); "So also my heavenly Father will deal with every one of you if you do not freely forgive your brother from your heart hid offenses".

James 2:13(KJV); "For to him who has shown no mercy the judgment [will be] merciless, but mercy [full of glad confidence] exults victoriously over judgment."

5. Despising the law: Follow the law whether it's from God or man.

    Pr. 28:9 (KJV); "He who turns his ear away from hearing the law [of God and man], even his prayer is an abomination, hateful and revolting to God".

    There are many laws in this world that we disagree with and feel we should not adhere to because we believe by obeying them we will be serving two masters. But God wants us to obey those laws set by the Government. Most laws are written to protect us. Take the laws away and I guarantee we would have anarchy. There are some people in this country and world that believe we should do away with governments. Just think of what would happen if we had no government and laws to protect us. Could the Government be the restrainer?

6. Blood –guiltiness: If you have not asked forgiveness of your sins you are still a sinner and you need to be washed by the blood of Jesus. He will wash you white as snow. You can ask forgiveness and God will honor your request, but if you continue to sin and live the old life [old man] compared to the new life [new man] God will not listen to your prayers. If you don't obey you can't pray.

Isaiah chapter 1 (KJV): Isaiah was concerned about the people of Israel and their iniquities toward God. He says in verse 4, "Ah sinful nation, a people laden with iniquity, a seed of evildoers, children that are corrupters: they have forsaken the Lord, they have provoked the Holy One of Israel unto anger; they have gone away backwards". Read and study the whole chapter and you will understand that they were being disobedient to God. Disobedience during the Old and New Testament are the same. Disobedience caused the first sin and the fall of our first parents which was spiritual death. God still regards disobedience to Him a sin. Don't believe that grace will be your protector. Some believe that grace will protect them from all sin, but they better take another look at what God meant when His Son Jesus died for our sins. Some forget what salvation really means. It doesn't mean its okay to continue sinning. It means a new birth of spiritual life. The Holy Spirit and you in the new man will win the battle and you will stop sinning. Remember it was God's grace to allow His Son to become a man, suffer and die on the Cross for our sins. If He didn't do that, we would still be living under the Old Testament laws. We might be getting away with our sinning today, but the day of God's Judgment is coming. We can not continue down that slippery slope of greasy grace. If we continue down this path, God will do the following.

Is.1:15-16 (KJV); "And when ye spread forth your hands, I will hide mine eyes from you: yea, when you make many prayers, I will not hear: cease to do evil. Wash you, make you clean; put away the evil of your doings from before mine eyes; cease to do evil".

Here is some advice to everyone. If you think you have God's word all figured out and you know the time and dates of everything that will happen, you better stop and think again. If God wanted us to know all of these things, why didn't He just put all of that information in the Bible so there would be no confusion in mans interpretation? God knew man was smart enough to figure things out, but, there is no mathematical equation to give us the answer. When He says no man will know until that day, that is what He meant. Today most denomination has their own interpretation of God's word and they would say they are right. Some may be similar but still different. Are we all setting under false doctrines? If I say that the Holy Spirit showed me the truth and it doesn't agree with other interpretations of His word, I'd better pray and take another look and ask God for conformation. People, who don't study God's word and just take the word of other people for a particular doctrine, should take a serious look at what they are agreeing with. Do what I'm doing by praying and asking God to show you the truth. He will allow His Holy Spirit to show you the truth because He is the truth.

CHAPTER SEVENTEEN

SECULAR PSYCHOLOGY

The question: can we use secular psychology to help the Christian family and church?

MY OPINION:

Most of my adult life I have been interested in people, how they think, work, behave, and react to negative and positive things. I am not a professional when it comes to human behavior, but after supervising people for 50+ years I feel I know some things about their behavior. As a supervisor/manager my belief has always been to tell the truth when evaluating a person's performance. I believed when you tell the truth it helps the person when and if improvement is needed. If their performance is good/ great positive reinforcement is necessary. No politics or favors played. In 1986 I read about a program developed by clinical psychologist that deals with human behavior, so I took this course that lasted for two and a half weeks. I spent many hours attending this teaching seminar and many more hours studying to pass the course. This was very educational in terms of learning how to better deal with people and help improve productivity in the work place. The instructors were Clinical Psychologist and they taught on how to improve quality and productivity in the work place through positive reinforcement. I was not completely convinced that everything being taught was correct in terms of dealing with people. I understand developing this type of program takes time and study by some very smart people, but I also understand it is necessary to spend some time dealing with people in the work place and their problems on a daily basis. I do believe this system of dealing with people is good for some but not all.

They developed a system of using the ABC approach to help managers understand how to deal with people. I shared some of this in another chapter, but think its' necessary to share again. It is a scientific data- based system for understanding human behavior. The book was written primarily for business use, but they say whether it's that of another or one's own behavior the principles of knowing human behavior are valid in all situations in which a person is trying to change a behavior. There is a lot more to understanding human behavior then just understanding the ABC'S. I can't go in to all the other things used to help improve human behavior because it would take another book. I think a similar type psychology was used by Norman Vincent Peal called the "Power of Positive Thinking". I think it is also being used by some ministers today. I believe they all lack a balance in dealing with human behavior in some respect. I will admit we humans lack complementing and giving positive reinforcement to others most of the time. We give more negative remarks to individuals and don't know how to correct a bad situation in a positive way. Then there are politics. The work place is loaded with political people who would use some of this to their advantage and not really helping the people in a positive way. This is where the lack of balance comes in. The truth needs to be told whether its' negative or positive and deal with correcting the problem. I believe if you don't tell a person the truth when they need help, it will not help them improve.

I believe this system was pioneered by Dr. B. F. Skinner. If used in the business world, it is a way to help get people to do what you want them to do. If used in a family situation the same positive results can happen. I am not a psychologist, but my personal opinion is there is some lack of balance in how to improve some behavior. By never telling people anything but positives about what they are doing could develop a character that could cause psychological problems when facing a negative in their life. I believe this has happened in our secular society and spilled over to our Christian society for the last thirty to forty years and caused some of the problems we see today. It has become a "ME" society. You might hurt their self-esteem if you tell them the truth. I recommend everyone read "The Vanishing Conscience" by John Macarthur. He explains that secular psychologist are creating a no fault society by telling you not to feel guilty for anything you do. He is right, society is slowly trying to do away with our conscience and if we don't change this we will die as a country. All of the crimes we see in our society today are because of the lack of mans conscience. Some people who murder and rob think its okay because they believe they can do as they please without feeling guilty. This is where our society has brought us by telling our children they are the best and never tell them if they have a problem.

Anyhow there are some positive uses for this type of psychology, even in the Christian society. We do lack positive reinforcement with others. I used some of what I was taught for comparing Christians and non-Christians in their behaviors. We are human with a mixture of different types of personalities, so you can't please everyone all the time. One of the things their psychology teaches is not to spend a lot of time on people personalities, which I believe has more to do with performance then positive reinforcement. Society whether secular or Christian is lacking the understanding of different personalities that people have. Did you ever listen to someone speaking about a subject close to your heart and their opinion is completely different than yours and you couldn't understand why? This could be the lack of knowledge about the subject or a different personality. Why do we think differently than other people? Could it be our personality? When I was in the work force I found that some personalities didn't want to be positively reinforced. Just leave them alone and let them do their work made them happy. Trying to put a system like this into action in the business world is very difficult unless it is a new business and all the people are young. This still doesn't guarantee a positive result with everyone.

I have made observations in the business and Christian world trying to understand people personalities and I found

SAMUEL D. SCULL

that you can change some people's character in the business world by using positive reinforcement, but not many. This is different in the Christian world. The only thing that can change it in the Christian world is accepting Jesus Christ as your savior and go through the born again experience. When this happens, your character becomes an automatic change to the positive. If you do not change you better get serious and go back to the altar. Believe me I have seen this happen many times. I don't care whether you're a blue, green, red, or yellow personality you become a new person. I've also seen people who were in a backslidden condition and their character changed for the worse because of a carnal state. God will let you go until you make up your own mind. I could always tell a true Christian in the business world because they always walked around with a smile and most of them were very productive. If one is not productive it was because they were not taught God's word, about working for you're wages. If you only show it in your talk and not your walk you better go back to the Alter and get serious.

The psychology of pushing your beliefs about your religion on your children or other people is wrong unless you show them what you're saying is the absolute truth. We should never take mans word as gospel. It takes study, prayer and discussion to make sure it is God's truth and not our opinion. There should be agreement between all Christians about God's word, not hundreds of churches with each one with their own interpretation. My mother raised me and my siblings in church, but never tried to brain wash any of us by pushing religion every minute of the day. I remember having many discussions with her about things being said

232

by ministers from the pulpit that I couldn't find in God's word. My mother was like most Christians being taught by people who said they were teaching the truth about God's word when after a period of time she found out some things being said was not the truth. Even though some teaching might not have been factual it still taught high standards and morals strait from the Bible. I believe the framers of our constitution did the same by using the Bible as their guide to set high standards and morals. These are slowly being done away with and our Government is getting more corrupt as time passes.

When reading and studying the history of the Christian movement in this country over the years, one has to ask the following question. Why does a Christian want to be involved in the secular political system? Our political system in this country appears to be so corrupt, why would Christians want to be involved? Our political system (government) in this country over the years has slowly become so large that it would be very difficult to reduce it in size. I do believe there are some people with strong convictions about having a small Government if given a chance they will reduce it in size. Most of the time the rhetoric is all political promises (lies) to get elected. Then I remembered God gave man a free will of his own. We need to remember that in this country our government was originally established by people that wanted to be free which also meant the freedom of religion. We do have many freedoms in this country according to our constitution, but with such a diverse religious belief system in our country today many lawmakers and Judges are being forced to interpret our freedoms differently.

SAMUEL D. SCULL

The bottom line is whether we can use secular psychology in the Christian family and church. The answer is yes, as long as it is done at the human level and not the spiritual level. We are all human and have personalities and react to things in a different way. We are creatures of habit which can be changed if we want change. The best way to make sure we are where we should be and create the balance that is necessary to live your life by is to give your life to Jesus Christ. Once you do this His Holy Spirit will enter and make sure the balance is there. Just remember you have to want this, so be serious and accept salvation, the miracle of God.

We do have another alternative and that is using the best psychologist we will ever meet and this person is supernatural in nature. When Jesus Christ ascended back to the Father he left His Holy Spirit with us to guide and teach us in all things. This becomes a spiritual part of our human life. We are so use to using our human intellect to do things, we forget when we become Christians we should start using our spiritual intellect. The reason we don't use our spirit that is now connected to God's Spirit is because we are afraid of the supernatural. We are afraid that control of our lives will be taken away from us and our human intellect will die. This is the war we humans are fighting every day. We need to die to the flesh and resurrect the spirit. If we can do this I will rule out the use for secular psychology in our churches because God will be in control, not man.

CHAPTER EIGHTEEN

RESPONSIBLILY

What is the Christians responsibility today?

I read an article recently about what some Christians call church today "The New Church" with a "New Jesus" because of what has and is still happening. The burnings and killings that we have seen in our Educational Institutions are now happening in our churches. A surprise, I don't think so. Christians in this country need to get their heads out of the sand, and wake up to the fact that we helped create this problem. We humans have a difficult time admitting our mistakes until it's either too late or impossible to correct. As I've said in another chapter I am not a psychologist, but I do see and understand things we humans do right and wrong. Right and wrong comes from teaching our children the differences between the two according to God's word. Our laws are written using what is right or wrong. So, the secular and Christian worlds pretty much see it the same.

You can discuss or decide what you believe is right or wrong according to some laws, but I believe most people know the difference. When you analyze the different societies and the different religions in this world, you'll find out people are taught a different philosophy having to do with human morals, character, and behavior having to do with what is right or wrong. But most governments around the world pretty much follow the same laws that this country does. I always went by this premise when raising my children, if you see things changing towards the worse, look for the root cause that made this happen, and correct it. Some parents have a mind set that their children never do anything wrong. We parents need to accept the truth and stick with it. Jesus said the truth will set you free. The truth will also bring a balance to people lives and that is lacking in our society today.

We need to return to being a strong nation under God, not a weak nation under man. Satan is in his glory when man takes control without God. Man has slowly taken complete control, whether in the government or in the church. The bible says God is in control through the power of His Holy Spirit. I don't mean that man should just sit back and let God do it all. I mean that man needs to pray and ask God how to do it properly, and then man can do it with the leading of His Holy Sprit. God wants Christians to be obedient and follow His commands. Of course, man always thinks he can do it better. There are many pastors, evangelist, and teachers today that would tell you, they are in control of the church, not the Holy Spirit. I hope they mean on a human level and not spiritual level.

The courts in our country are slowly doing away with our Christian values by allowing some that don't share our Christian belief, to come in and concentrate on doing away with everything having to do with God and our Christian way of living. Do we know what the constitution says about our freedoms? If we were born in this country and don't know, we should. A high percentage of non-citizens and illegal immigrants and new citizens in this country probably know more about our constitution than the average citizen that was born here. Instead of the ACLU and others making sure citizens in this country are well versed on the constitution, they are out there trying to make citizens out of illegal immigrants, removing all things having to do with Christianity out of our Government buildings, including our schools. This is being allowed by people we elect and appoint to represent, protect, and serve us. There are many people around the world who would rather do away with the Christian way of living, rather than joining and trying to make the world a more peaceful and safe place to live. The direction this country is going in will be its downfall. Missionaries will be coming from abroad to this country to remind us where we came from and I believe this is already happening.

The same goes for the Bible (our constitution written by God) in respect to knowing and understanding what it says, not someone telling you what it says and means. Read it and study it for yourself. We are not living in times when we would be put to death for even having a Bible in our possession. It did happen in the past, and still happens in some countries around the world, but not in this country,

SAMUEL D. SCULL

as of yet. If we believe in God and the Bible is His written Word, we need to read it, and listen to what Christian teachers have to say, and then ask the Holy Spirit to help you put His word into proper context. After doing so, compare it with things happening around the world today, especially in the church. We read about ministers around the world saying they don't need the Christian church in the United States to continue sending missionaries. Why? Because they believe we have thrown the Holy Spirit out, and now are letting man take control. I shared what these ministers were saying with a pastor where we were attending church, and he got upset with me. He said, he really didn't care what the ministers around the world think, they were wrong. Just prior to our discussion he made a statement in a Bible study group saying he was in control at his church, not the Holy Spirit.

I know that I am not the only one that sees and understands what is going on in the Christian church today. I'm sharing this because most ministers will not. The church has forgotten who is in charge. Man has taken control of the church and kept it for so long, they have become complacent. They have forgotten that God is still in control. Some ministers forget about some leaders in the Bible that forgot who was in control and their outcome. They better take a step back and pray that God will re-open their eyes before it's too late. It's no wander small churches are empty of people and the mega churches are full. Ministers in the mega churches are teaching the feel good message to keep the money flowing in, not the souls. Billy Graham had Crusades in large Stadiums which cost lots of money and he didn't pull any punches when it came to preaching the whole (not watered down) Gospel. Salvation was his ministry and he stuck with it. Some small churches are being run by politicians, not telling the truth, and using mans gimmicks to increase attendance. Some churches don't even know what an alter call is, and can't take time to talk to God because they don't know how. Some don't know what it is to have a conversation with God. When people are burdened with trials, they don't understand why God don't jump in and lift the burden right away. The reason is they don't really understand God. We have to pray, read His word, study, and put things into context before understanding God.

My observation is that everyone wants a piece of the action and the action is not God. It's money! It appears like some ministers want to talk about today is mega churches and how much money they bring in. What happened to people being called by God that are more interested in mans soul then how big the church is and how much money is coming in. Christians need to start praying that these crooks, hiding behind a sheep's wool will be cut off from the Body of Christ. Christians need to pray for the real man of God to come in and take over, allowing the Holy Spirit to take control. The Holy Spirit knows what to do, and if we are listening to Him, everything will fall in line. If we want to see great things happen, keep the Holy Spirit in and throw the old man satan out. This includes the political old man.

There are some difference between the church today and when it was established at the day of Pentecost. At the day of Pentecost the people worshiped God night and day and in unity. This does not mean we have to be at the Wailing Wall

SAMUEL D. SCULL

all the time. It means we should have God in our thoughts at all times, fellowshipping with Him. The disciples taught the truth and didn't leave anything out. Some ministers are using psychology and political ways today to control things in the church and are afraid to teach the truth. Why? They're afraid people will leave the church and there goes the membership and tithes. I strongly believe too much emphasis is put on money and membership today and not enough put on salvation missions. The mega churches are taking away from the small church. I believe if some of the millions of dollars that mega churches make were reinvested in small churches in America it would help them stay above board to survive. At the rate were going the mega church will be the only church and people will have to sit home in front of their television to here God's word because the small church could not afford to stay open. I remember when ministers depended on God to provide for them and never failed to do so. Where has the trust in God gone? Trust or greed, which is it?

God's gifts were given for the edifying and building up of the Body of Christ. Today, theses same gifts are being used to edify individuals and feed their egos. The gifts are being used for personal gains and most of the time they are taken out of context. God gave us a way to test the prophets as they did in Christ time. We have that same authority according to His word, but ministers today will not let that happen. Why? Because there is probably something wrong in Denmark. You know what I mean, secrets or wrong doings. I believe there are so many false teachers (ministers) in the Christian church today it would blow our minds if we new the truth and who they were.

I remember one incident in a church I was attending. God had showed me according to His word that some people in the church were out of order and taking God's word out of context. This was not only happening in this church but a lot of other churches. I explained this to the Pastor, shared, and showed it to him in God's word. The Pastor accepted what I showed him and discussed it with the people involved. Of course this was against the doctrine they were ministering under and become a problem for not only the Pastor, but also the people who had been doing these things out of order for many years. It did stop for a short period of time, but continued when I wasn't there. Even though the Pastor acknowledged my gift, it made him nerves because he knew that God was showing me other things being done that were not according to His word. I won't go in to detail, but my time attending the church ended.

There have been so many changes in all churches over the years and most of these changes have to do with different interpretations of God's word. It has went from God being in control to man being in control. I know of at least five churches that have split because of fear and paranoia from the leadership. God has also showed me a few pastors that have failed in their calling because they went outside of their calling. Man's ego gets the best of him/her and that is when they start down the wrong road (their road), not God's. In Christian society today some ministers have taken their eyes off God and are looking for what the Jones(neighbors) have and they want it to. So instead of doing what God called them for, they start down the road of greed on their own.

My wife and I didn't attend church for a few years because we had a difficult time with politicians taking control, and taking the church in the wrong direction. When returning we ask this question of three ministers. What happened to all the young people? There were only a few in two churches that we attended? The answer from all three, they didn't know. This was hard for us to understand why they didn't know because they were in control for all those years. This was like asking a school teacher why your son or daughter is failing a subject and they say to you, they don't know. You first thought would be, the teacher is incompetent, and then you would have your child moved to another class. Is this what happened to all the young people in our churches? Did the ministers lose their way and the outcome was they lost all the young people? If you don't know why the young people left, you're either covering something up, or maybe you're in the wrong position. A person called by God to fill this very important position and is doing what God wants them to do, not what they want to do, should know everything that is going on in their church at all times. It sounds to me like we better get back to where we started, ask God's forgiveness and start all over with a fresh look at where we are, and where God wants us to go. Maybe the real problem is, they were in control, and not God, and they didn't want to admit it.

I wrote this book because God has given me answers to questions I've had for many years. I finally awakened to the fact that God talks to all born again Christians. His son

Jesus made this happen when He took the stripes on His back, and died on the cross for our sins. Now, all Christians have the same opportunity. We can go to Him for council, with our questions and concerns, wanting to do what he commands. He sent His Holy Spirit to do His work, and be our comforter, and guide. When Biblical scholars are ask questions, some of the answers I receive never seem to match what I've read and understand about God's word. God says to study and show thyself approved, meaning, don't just listen to the teacher or preacher, but read, and study the word, discussing it with others who are doing the same. Put your heart knowledge before your head knowledge and you will be going down the right path to the truth.

CHAPTER NINETEEN

REVIVAL

REFLECTION ON "REAL" REVIVAL

The church is always looking for revival and for many reasons, but sometime the wrong reasons. The many reasons could be, spiritual, membership, leaders, truth, money, new building, etc, etc, some good, some bad.

I read a religious article written by a local Minister in the news paper some time ago that concerned me, so I ask God to help me understand what it really meant. After praying about what this Minister was saying I ask God to help me reflect on the article by writing how I understood what His word says about revival and sending it to the news paper. I responded by writing an article and to make a long story short my article was never published. Why? I don't know. I tried to contact the news paper people several times with no success. So I decided to write about it in this book. Anyhow his article was about a scheduled revival in a local church on a certain date. This was a scheduled revival by man as some ministers do with healing and prophecy meetings. In some healing meetings they decide who will be healed and give people a certain time to be on stage. It's like being in a Doctors office, or a movie, or a ball game, or a car repair shop for a scheduled time or appointment. I always thought God would say when a revival will happen by using His Holy Spirit to prepare people through His conviction.

This is the article I wrote reflecting on the Pastors article with names and addresses removed. This is not the entire article, but, important things he says and some added emphasis by me.

ARTICLE

Being part of the church (body of Christ) I would like to reflect on an article written by a Pastor in a local church. [The heading of his article read, "Don't you think it's about time for a **real** revival".] What I'm about to share is not pointing the finger or criticizing anyone, it's my opinion. My opinion is how I believe man has taken control of a responsibility that was given to the Holy Spirit by the Father. I would like to complement the Pastor on being honest about a problem that has plagued the church for years and people have been afraid to discuss it. As a layman and someone that has attended church most of my life I would like to reflect on what the Pastor said. The Pastor statements are in the brackets.

[The Pastor said we need a **real** revival.] I will agree we do need a revival in the church (body of Christ). But what does he mean by **real**? Is he saying all revivals have not been **real**, or was he saying there is something wrong with the way some leaders say their church is having a revival and after a couple of weeks they are right back where they started, spiritually dead? God has showed me over the years that most revivals are held for the wrong reason, not for the renewal of spirit, but for the increase in membership and tithes. Maybe the revivals in the past have been for selfish reasons only and we know God will not participate in anything false.

[The Pastor also states the church (body of Christ) has been dying and needs to be brought back to life.] I wholeheartedly agree. The dying church didn't just happen. It started years ago when man (meaning all humans) decided to take control of everything by taking the reins away from the one who needs to have control, and we all know who that is, the one Jesus said he would send, His Holy Spirit. The church has put Him aside and man decides what happens in the church. This sounds like the kingdom of the world, not the Kingdom of God. Ministers in Europe, Africa, and other countries are now saying what the church in America is missing is the Holy Spirit. Some ministers in America would disagree, but those are the ones that are trying to win people for God with man's gimmicks and not God's word. When the church finally recognizes what they are doing wrong and returns control to the Holy Spirit we will all walk in the spirit and will not have any interest in fulfilling the lust of the flesh.

[Again, the Pastor is right when he says we have failed to prepare God's people for the works of service.] I've shared this with a few Pastors and they agree, but nothing ever changes. There is too much emphasis put on money and membership and not enough on educating people in God's word. Some play the political game, only concentrating on the ones they believe will help them with gimmicks that will increase tithes and membership. People are more interested in receiving a political position in the church organization or bragging about their education than they are about educating other Christians about God's word which would help increase God's Kingdom, not theirs. Like I said, I believe in education but not bragging about it, or using it to lord over people. Some personalities have a difficult time dealing with their education.

Some think having church on Sundays is enough and weekly bible studies are not necessary. How many people who go to church really know how to share the salvation message or understand how the church is to be organized? When I ask biblical questions about God's word it's amazing how some ministers differ in their interpretation of certain scriptures. After analyzing what they are saying I am convinced they are only interpreting man's doctrine, not God's. Some ministers have a difficult time agreeing with their denominational doctrine and also have a difficult time explaining it. As a Christian nation we know less about Christianity than most people know in other nations about their religion. Attending church today is more like a social gathering instead of spirit gathering. It is like a political gathering of liberals, conservatives and a few independents. The leadership will give the good old hand shake or slap on the back to who they think can be won over to their side of any problem in the church they have caused.

[The Pastor gives reference to Eph. 4:11-13 (KJV) about who Jesus appoints as leaders and their responsibilities.] I suggest we all re-read the whole chapter because we sometimes forget all the other scriptures are important and should all be put into context. Remember it is Jesus who appoints, not man. [He ask, "Who are the people responsible for killing Gods' church" and he received an answer, "everything rises and falls on leadership."] I agree. I will say this, all problems that arise in the church are not always caused by the leadership, but there is a fair amount and most of the time no blame is accepted by them. When I ask the leadership why is the church attendance down the answer is always, "I don't know". You soon find out they did know, but didn't want too talk about it or admit it might be their fault. It is time for leadership to get off their high horse and take personal responsibility for their actions and start asking the Holy Spirit to give them guidance, instead of man.

Many reasons can be given for why God is not present in some churches, such as people playing politics for leadership positions or stacking the membership for elections to favor one side, big egos (self pride that wants everything their way or else), losing control (someone else trying to take control), lack of Godly fear, and to much human fear, to much arrogance, to much intellect (head knowledge), and not enough heart knowledge etc. [The Pastor goes on and talks about being politically correct when praying for others.] We need to get out of politics with other Christians and stop trying to use our intellect to make things happen and start using our heart with love, God's love.

God has shown me in the past that the truth needs to be told and I am beginning to see and hear this from some ministers and laymen that are not afraid to speak up. Some pastors have reached a point in their ministry where fear has taken over to tell the truth about God's word. Some ministers are now saying to the laymen, only laymen can tell the whole story about God's word and get away with it. Some ministers are afraid to quote and discuss certain scriptures with the congregation because they might disagree, so fear sets in and the minister fears he/she could loose their position as pastor, or some might leave the church. I say to them, this looks like mans fear. If God calls you in to the ministry, why should you fear if you are sharing God's word and telling the truth? We fail God if we don't teach the whole Bible. We either believe the whole Bible or we don't. If we don't, we are in the wrong business. Why are we afraid to teach the whole truth? Christians today want to hear a feel good message and not the truth. Ministers who say they have been called by God, need to stand up, show God's power in their life, and tell the whole story, not just what they think people want to hear. They might find out people want to hear the truth, especially those who are serious about living for God. The Holy Spirit will deal with the political people who want to control things in the church.

God is calling all people to repent and especially leaders along with all who participate in leadership rolls in the church. We need to be the roll models as Jesus was while here on earth. This means make it our daily routine to talk the talk and walk the walk as He did, and become mature in the word, which will help us not do things as the enemy does. God's word says we are born again, the old man dies and the new man emerges, and should never look back. When you look back, the old man (satan) keeps tugging and continues his attempts to win you back to his evil empire.

THE REVIVAL OF OUR SPIRIT SHOULD BE HAPPENING EVERYDAY, NOT ONLY WHEN THE CHURCH DECIDES IT'S TIME FOR A REVIVAL. READING GOD'S WORD, PRAYING, AND ASKING HIM EVERYDAY TO KEEP OUR SPIRIT RENEWED WILL HELP US HAVE CONSTANT REVIVAL IN OUR LIVES. GOD DID NOT MAKE US PUPPETS SO HE COULD CONTROL US, HE WANTS US TO TAKE PART AND BE SERIOUS ABOUT IT THROUGH LOVE. IT'S TIME WE CHRISTIANS STOP ACTING LIKE PEOPLE IN THE OLD TESTAMENT AND BECOME SERIOUS NEW TESTAMENT FOLLOWERS OF CHRIST.

REMEMBER, POLITICS AND HYPOCRISY ARE NOT WAYS TO REACH TO GOD.

REAL REVIVAL WILL DRAW PEOPLE UNTO GOD VIA HIS HOLY SPIRIT AND WE WILL NOT HAVE TO ADVERTIZE IT IN THE NEWS PAPER. NEWS OF THE REVIVAL WILL BE SHARED BY CHRISTIANS. IT IS CALLED SHARING THROUGH THE HOLY SPIRIT. WE MIGHT BE SURPRISED WHEN WE TAKE GOD SERIOUS AND START SHARING HIS WORD HOW THE HOLY SPIRIT WILL START TOUCHING PEOPLES LIVES, PEOPLE WE DON'T EVEN KNOW.

CHAPTER 20

SERIOUS OR NOT

ARE WE SERIOUS ABOUT CHRISTIANITY AND THE TRUTH OR DO WE JUST PLAY CHURCH?

What I really mean about being serious is this, do Christians want to know the truth or is it just politics as usual? Is it a social gathering to discuss politics, vacations, family problems, sports etc, or is it for fellowship, worship, learning, and discussing God's word?

In the U.S.A, there are a growing number of laypeople and ministers that recognize there is a change in how Christians worship God, especially the youth. My family and I attended a church for a short period of time and it appeared to be a training ground for sporting events. Some worship services were more like being at a football game with young girls (cheerleaders) line up dancing, and cheering, and others with their musical instruments so loud it would hurt your ear drums. The minister condoned this kind of behavior and got upset when I approached him about the situation. His feeling was if we let the youth do as they please, even though it was fake, it would keep them in church. We know football players, band people, and cheerleaders have to be trained how to perform, but is that the way we want to worship God? It appears as though young Christians today have to be trained in ways not found in the scriptures to worship the heavenly Father. I can't remember any loud music, cheerleading, or trained dancing when I was growing up in church.

I did observe the Holy Spirit working in peoples lives as talked about in Acts. The Holy Spirit was in control, not man. We forget that God is not hard of hearing. The church was always full of people that were serious about his word and respected His Sanctuary for worship. God is a God to be respected through our worship and we need to make sure we are doing that. We don't need training in how to worship God. The Holy Spirit will help and guide us, if we listen. The Holy Spirit will work in supernatural ways if we give Him a chance. The worship services are now lead by a "ME" generation. It's all about the "ME" syndrome. Who helped develop this in our youth? Let's start with Mom and Dad being sucked in by the secular society. Our secular society has passed laws they thought was needed to help parents better raise their children. Doctors have convinced parents how to deal with their children's self-esteem. We have allowed the secular society to take over raising our children. Because of this, parents have convinced their children that they are the greatest thing that ever walked this earth, even if they are not. There are many problems developing in the youth today because of this unbalanced way of raising them. It has come down to everyone competing for the top spot and if you don't make it there, it's time for the psychologist. The medical society is making millions to help the youth deal with their self-esteem and trying their best to make people believe it's not their fault. It is called the no fault society.

In some churches there are at least five to seven singers and three/six people with instruments leading worship. I wonder what would happen if the minister asked them to sit down, worship God, be fed the word, learn about God, and have one person lead the worship service with a piano/organ. Would they stay, leave, or not return the following week? I'll let you guess. I believe the lack of teaching a balance from His word has caused people to misunderstand who is in charge. We are being told by ministers that we need to be trained in how to dance, cheer (like at a sports game), beat drums, and sing so loud you can't understand the words or even hear others worshiping. This is all being organized by man and not God through His Holy Spirit. Why?

It appears that two to three generations of young people have stopped or not even thought about going to church. Some of the youth that stayed and some new young converts have brought the secular way of doing things into the church. When ministers are asked what happened to all these missing youth, the answer is, they don't know. NOT KNOWING WHAT IS GOING ON UNDER YOUR RESPONSIBILTY AS A PASTOR IS NOT A GOOD ANSWER. The head of a flock of Christians not knowing why they left or attend is like a Shepherd of a flock of sheep saying he lost the heard and he doesn't know why or where they are. HOW SERIOUS CAN MINISTERS BE?

Is being called by God and accepting the call suppose to be serious or just another routine job? It appears like ministers have lost their way and now they want complete control of everything in the church. They are trying to justify what has happened to all the people and hopefully save their job. They are changing the way God wants us to worship Him by pushing on the people how they want them to worship. A minister in a Pentecostal church told me he would get together with other ministers of the same doctrine and practice how to speak in tongues and give interpretation. I would like for them to show me where to find that in the scriptures. This sounds like the time when I was growing up and the ministers and elders of the church started coaching me how to receive the Baptism in the Holy Spirit. Not scriptural! I can't read anywhere in the scriptures where Jesus had the Apostles practice how to speak in another language. When the apostles were filled with the Holy Spirit on the day of Pentecost and spoke in tongues, they weren't coached. This sounds more like man controlling what happens and not the Holy Spirit. THIS IS THE PROBLEM!!! Man is slowly loosing his faith in God or letting his intellect take control and forgetting who is really in charge.

As I read the Bible my understanding is, God created everything and He is the one and only God. He created man to fellowship with and he was a disappointment. Man continues to disappoint God and will continue to until the end of time. Man is born in sin and this makes him weak and when born again through salvation it makes him strong. It's time we return to the truth by putting things into context. God created man, sent his son Jesus to save us all from our sins. He died on the cross and was resurrected and returned to the right hand of the Father. He sent a comforter in His place to guide and comfort us by His word. He is in us and if we listen to Him and follow His guidance we can do anything according to His will.

God the Father and Son are in Heaven, waiting for us to utilize what has been given to us and that is the Holy Spirit. He is in charge, not man. We will wake up one of these days and return control to Him. It is God's spirit in us and not our spirit that has control. We have a difficult time understanding that. The church has drifted so far away from center (Jesus being the center) it will have a difficult time returning back to balance (telling the whole truth).

Christians continue to say they understand what the Bible says, and they know the difference between heaven and hell, but, still walk the fence between obedience and disobedience. Remember, God wants full obedience (not partial) as he did from the beginning. He will not accept disobedience, so don't believe because we live under grace in New Testament times you can straddle the fence. Who was obedient? Christ was, and where did He go after suffering for the disobedient people? He went back to the Right Hand of the Father. Remember Jesus being a human had a free will just as everyone had and still does. He could have decided not to go through the torture and God could have destroyed mankind. But, because of His obedience, and atoning for our sins, saved us all, and still is allowing us to make our own decision between Heaven and hell. I prefer to spend eternal life in Heaven and not eternal life in hell. Do you want to take that chance?

Obedience to God is one of the most important aspects of knowing and understanding Him. The Ancient One created all things and only asks man to be obedient. That should have been an easy task, but man decided to take it upon himself to disobey. I will try to show you why man is still disobedient to God.

God is perfect and made man in His likeness. Our first parents were both innocent and knew no wrong. They were placed in the Garden of Eden to maintain it and had dominion over all things on earth. God gave them rules concerning what they could and could not eat in the Garden. He set the stage to test man's obedience and both Adam and Eve failed. By disobeying God's rules, they caused all mankind to take sin into their hearts. God did this to show man that he had a choice and the difference between right and wrong. He wanted man to know he was free to make his own choices and not a robot controlled by Him. We all know the wrong choice was made. Prior to sin entering into our lives, man with his Godlike mind, needed no conscience, but surely needed it after sin entered in to determine right from wrong.

As you study the Old Testament, God continued to look for men with trusting obedience to Him, starting with Abel's offering and Enoch's trust and the people still continued their disobedience. God continued to find great men such as, Noah, Abraham and Moses who showed trusting obedience to Him. The Old and New Testament reveals many people with trusting obedience to God, but something has happened to trusting obedience through the centuries since the time of Jesus.

Disobedience started with Adam and Eve, continued through time and still continues today. When God sent His Son to redeem us, He created an opportunity to stand before God in a righteous state. We still do not understand that He wants us to be fully obedient. We have a difficult time understanding what full obedience actually means. It doesn't mean partial it means full obedience to Him. Christians today still think partial obedience is satisfactory. Read 1 Samuel 15 (KJV), Saul's obedience was partial because he didn't complete God's commands. As commanded, he killed all the people, but "he captured Agag, the King of the Amalekites alive." "Saul and the people spared Agag and the best of the sheep, oxen, fatlings, lambs, all that was good and were not willing to destroy them utterly; but everything despised and worthless, that they utterly destroyed."[1] Whatever his reasons, he disobeyed the clear command of God and allowed Agag to live. The sin was so serious that God immediately disposed Saul and his descendants from the throne of Israel. God said, "Because you have rejected the work of the Lord, He has also rejected you from being king of Israel." There are many scriptures throughout the Bible like this and as time passes by, we are committing the same disobedience to God.

We cannot obey partially or halfheartedly as we seek to eliminate sin from our lives. We cannot stop while the task remains incomplete. Sinners, such as the Amalekites, have a way of escaping the slaughter, breeding, reviving, regrouping and launching new and unexpected assaults on our most vulnerable areas. God's Word is based on obedience. All things done in the past, present and future are in obedience by Faith. All the great people of the Bible received God's blessing by being obedient to Him and when disobedient, saw His wrath. What makes us think we are different? Many churches today are concerned about the decline of obedience to God in born-again Christians. Today's Christian appears to be losing interest in God's way of doing things and because of this the body of Christ is suffering. As time passes on and everyone appears to be comfortable in their Christian walk around the world, disobedience seems to increase. It follows the trend people took in the Old and New Testaments. The scriptures say, "Whatsoever we ask, we receive of Him because we keep His commandments, and do these things which are pleasing in His sight." In other words, if we expect God to do as we ask Him, we must do whatever God bids us to do by having a listening ear for a listening ear. On the other hand, if we turn a deaf ear, He will likely turn a deaf ear to us. Obeying God's commandments are not difficult to follow. He created us in His image and made us without sin. Remember, Adam caused all generations to be disobedient to God.

I will attempt to show you that our need for obedience to God today has not changed or diminished since the time of Adam. I will also try to show you this is one of the reasons we are not seeing revival, healings, miracles and God's Holy Spirit moving among Christians at all times. If we give God partial, we should expect partial or maybe nothing in return. Is this because of partial obedience to God?

Adam and Eve found out quickly the consequence of making the wrong decision. Now that there are two ways to choose, right or wrong, society appears to want the destructive way mainly because we live under God's grace. Secular society is looking for ways to help Christians circumvent being obedient to God by doing away with our conscience. It is evident that people in our culture are becoming very good at blame-shifting, making scapegoats of parents, childhood disappointments and other dysfunctions beyond our control.

If you suffer from a psychological disorder, whether you are a schizophrenic or just someone struggling with emotional distress, you can easily find someone to explain why you're problem is not your fault and teach you how to silence a troubled conscience. Instead of following God's Word by being obedient to His Commandments, we choose to do wrong and our conscience works on us until we look for man's way of solving the problem. Instead of praying and asking for God's help through His word and being obedient, we are helping society go down the wrong path.

From the begining of Christianity to the present day, it is difficult keeping up with human interpretations of the Scriptures. In the United States alone, it is almost impossible to decipher who is right or wrong in their teachings. Some respected Christian ministers are teaching it's not sin but your self-esteem that needs changing. They are also teaching that because it's in the Bible does not mean you have to teach or preach it, especially if it has to do with your conscience. I believe the born-again Christian is lacking the most important ingredient that would stop the decaying away of man's heart, "The Holy Spirit". Man's intellect tries its' best to control his life and that is where the trouble starts. We have allowed the secular society to become our conscience instead the Holy Spirit. We need to allow Him to do what He was sent here for. In order to make that happen, we must acknowledge Him and be obedient to the Word. Our God given conscience is working on sin in our lives and we are turning to the secular society to remove the guilt and not the sin.

The bottom line means we must stop separating sins by placing them in categories of importance. God says sin is sin no matter how small or large. God still wants us to be truly obedient. We need to take a good look at our lives and stop justifying any sin, asking the Holy Spirit to work on our conscience daily.

I'm saying all of this because I believe this is why God is not allowing the restrainer that holds back the anti-Christ to be removed, as of yet. I believe God is waiting and will not let this happen until we Christians start obeying. Jesus did not come to do away with the commandments. God is the same today as He's always been. It is because of His son's obedience that we still have a chance to make the right decision. God wants unity and a church without spot or wrinkle and the only way that will happen is through obedience. If you want things to happen, start being obedient, follow His commands, love one another, remind each other what a Christian is suppose to be and do daily, and insist that all ministers teach and preach the truth. Remember, iron sharpens iron.

The world understands what Christianity is, and some secular people can tell you all about the scriptures, and how the church has failed, because of allowing politics and hypocrisy to control it. Meaning, the church is being controlled by mans doctrine and not God's. Anyone called by God to fill an office listed in Eph. 4:10-11(KJV) knows the truth, but most fail to fulfill their calling because of politics within the body of Christ. When problems arise and strife enters some ministers decide they must take control and all of a sudden they know how to do things better then God. Some ministers/teachers and laypeople better wake up, start listening to the Holy Spirit, and start telling the truth, or get left behind.

I mentioned in another chapter about a phrase in some college material I was reading. It said "If you don't obey you can not pray". I believe this with all my heart. I believe that is what happened to most of the prophets in the Old Testament. Most tried there best to obey but missed the mark. Jesus is one that the Father was completely satisfied with and we should all be thankful for that. Ministers today are preaching a feel good message so people will stay put and pay their tithe. I hate to say this, but I believe money has become more important than teaching the truth. They want to be liked by all, including ministers and people from other denominations, even though they don't teach the same doctrines. Its okay to show Christian love as Jesus taught, but we should not share a doctrine we don't believe in. The Bible talks about false doctrine in, Is.32:6, Matt.16:12, Col. 2: 8 and He.13:9 (KJV). It also talks about false teachers, heresy, seducers, and deceivers. If we don't see them, we are blinded by the spirit of confusion.

Are we afraid of persecution and standing up for the truth? In 2 Tim. 3:12 (KJV) it says, "All who desire to live godly in Christ Jesus will suffer persecution. In John 15: 19-20 (KJV), Jesus said: "if the world hates you, you know that it hated Me before it hated you. If you were of the world, the world would love its own. Yet because you are not of the world, but I chose you out of the world, therefore the world hates you". Remember the word that I said to you, "A servant is not greater than his master." If they persecuted Me, they will also persecute you".

Are most Christians under religious persecution? You can answer that for yourselves. I will tell you what the Bible says and are we ready to standup for what God's word says? Are you ready to stand up to the Christian and non-Christian who don't believe the same as you, even though you can prove what you're saying from God's word? Are we out there telling the world that Jesus Christ is the Son of God, and not just some prophet, like Moses or John the Baptist. Jesus died for our sins, gives us a choice, and will return for His Bride, the church. There are millions, if not billions, that don't believe this, and are letting the world know it. Are they afraid to be persecuted for their beliefs? I don't think so, just look at what is happening in the Middle East with the Muslims and their Islam religion.

So, let's get **serious**, show your **faith** in God, and His Son, by stepping out and have **trust** that what it says in His Word is the **truth. It is trust that will make things happen, not** fear that it might not. Fear will negate your trust if you let it. When things start happening, remember, it is all for the glory of God, not you.

CONCLUSION

Things that we have written about in this book might seem frivolous to some, but not others. It might seem petty, only my opinion, but believe me, these kind of problems are keeping many churches cold and not very enticing to people who want to be obedient or sinners knowing something is missing in their lives. Some people steer clear because they understand all the hypocrisy going on inside and outside the walls. I believe what I've said is very important to Christians who belong to small community churches that want God in their lives. I don't want to address mega churches at this time because I suggest some of them are in it for reasons other than being disciples for Christ. Some people that attend mega churches like to hear the one sided gospel, you know, "everything is okay". If we continue down this road of man controlling everything without the guidance of the Holy Spirit the church (body of Christ) will never be in unity. We need to get serious, because satan and his friends are getting busy because they know the time is running out. His forces are growing around the world to defend him and his false teaching. Satan knows time is running out and he is working overtime to win souls. Are we? If ministers and all Christian leaders can't see what is happening, I would conclude they are spiritually blind. And if they do know and aren't willing to do anything about it, the Christian laymen should pray for God to replace them. If the church is set up like a secular political system, do what is said about secular political leaders when they don't do their jobs, don't re-elect them, elect new leaders that are willing to serve God and the people and tell the truth.

God has showed me that more new churches are not what are needed. There are so many churches in this country now that are closing or only have a handful of people. These buildings will hold millions of people. What are needed is obedience, dedication, and the willingness to live for God and do as the disciples did, become fishers of men. This means to study to show thyself approved, stop using politics to control the church and return control to the Holy Spirit. We need to show more of Christ in our lives by not only our talk, but in our **walk**. Our **walk** is just as important and sometime more effective then our talk.

We Christians need to get serious about being obedient to God's word and share with the leaders what God expects from all Christians, and that is what His word says. There are no perfect Christians, we all have sinned and come short of the glory of God. Jesus is the only perfect one and He saved us from our sins. What God is looking for are mature Christians that are willing to stand up for what His Son did for all humanity and not just for personal gain and what the secular world has. Christians continue to fall for satans tricks, luring them into believing they need everything the secular world has. I call this Christians trying to balance both sides and not really understanding how satan is conning them in to becoming hypocrites (sinning). We are walking a thin line between two worlds and the secular world seems to be winning. This war has been going on sense the beginning with satan and our first parents. We continue to make the same mistakes by being disobedient, knowing it is wrong. We need to learn from our mistakes by being obedient and get on God's side.

We also need to be like Christians should be when strife enters, whether in church or at home. Did you ever notice how some Christians react when someone leaves the church for what ever reason, and there are many? It doesn't matter why they left, but some Christians from the church meet them in the public and ignore them. Is this the way Christians should act? We Christians should always treat people as Christ did no matter who they are or what the circumstances may be. I could go on and on about how we Christians need to improve our lives, looking at ourselves, our talk and walk, to make sure it matches God's word. The most important thing needed is our relationship with our Father in Heaven. Are we still on talking terms with Him? If not, renew your relationship with Him by starting a conversation now. He will always take time to talk with you. Why? Because he still loves you

I hope you enjoyed the book. I might have said some things that some will not agree with, but that's life. I only want to share what I believe God is showing me and hopefully help people understand what we need as Christians to help move to unity in the body of Christ. A splintered body will not do it. You and I with the guidance of the Holy Spirit can make this happen. We need to give control back to God and allow His Holy Spirit to complete His assignment as Jesus did.

In Christ

ABOUT THE AUTHOR

My Christian walk has been very interesting. I have attended Pentecostal churches over the years. As other Christians believe, so do Pentecostals with the exception of a few doctrinal differences which most churches have. I believe there are churches that take some scriptures way out of context and boarder on the cult. After a few years of having concerns about things happening in the Pentecostal church I attended, I decided to get a degree in Bible Theology. I received an Associate Degree in the year of Two Thousand and One. I completed most of the necessary studies towards earning a Bachelors Degree. I but put my studies on hold to write this book. God was showing me and others the church was in a place of distress, so He wanted some people to start telling the whole story, not just the half story that some have decided to tell for many, many years. The reason for getting the education in Bible Theology is because of how our Christian society today requires you to have a College degree or people won't even listen to you. This is the mind set of the intellectuals in the world, especially in the United States.

I believe most people who are frequent readers look at the title of a book and who the author is before deciding to purchase it. There are many Christian authors that write very excellent books about God's word and I have read many of them. These authors are very well known and their books are read by millions. This is my first book and here is a short synopsis of my life.

I am not a famous person, just an average Joe, raised in a Christian family who loves the Lord. I use the vocabulary common people understand. During my lifetime as a Christian, while attending church, I sometimes had questions about things being taught, whether they were scriptural or just man's interpretation on how he wanted things done. This plagued me for many years and during the year of 2003 while I was studying God's word He called on me to write and teach the truth about His word. My teaching has been mostly in Bible study groups by sharing what God has showed me about His Word. Writing this book has been slow for many reasons but God told me to be patient. I have been for the last few years and continue to do so today, being exposed to God's church for over seventy years and God placing in my heart to tell people the whole truth and not partial truth about His word. Partial truth leads the way to unbalanced Christians. I believe because God ask me to do this He also gave me the qualifications necessary to write this book.

I grew up in a large family of five boys and two girls. My mother and father did their best to feed and raise a healthy family while struggling through part of the great depression and the World War II years with minimum income. We were poor, but happy. We were happy because we lived in a Christian atmosphere. Although we went through some bad times our Christian upbringing kept us going. I can't remember the family ever complaining about how bad times were. I guess it was because we were happy with everything we had and appreciated what our parents were doing to raise a large family in very trying times. To appreciate how well we have it in our society today we need to read more about how some people had to live prior to 1945. If our society today had to revert back and live as people did during those years there wouldn't be enough psychologist to handle the onslaught of people needing help.

In March of 1952, I convinced my Dad to sign government papers allowing me to join the Navy. I was seventeen and at that time in my life I believe this was the best thing for me. Of course my mother was not enthused about me leaving because of the Korean War. I joined the Navy and spent the next four years serving the American people during the War assigned to the U.S. Navy Atlantic Sixth Fleet. My time spent in the Navy was very educational and I met some very interesting people. I was in an honor guard on the U.S.S. Newport News that welcomed the King and Queen of Greece aboard. On occasions we had some VIP'S onboard like the Secretary of the Navy "Admiral Carney", Secretary of the Army "Omar Bradley", and Secretary of Defense "Wilson". We were scheduled to go to the Queen's Carination in 1952 in England, but, were redirected back to the States to take President Eisenhower, Prime Minister Churchill, and Stalin to a Big Three meeting in Bermuda and when we reached the Sates the meeting was canceled. I shared my time with many friends and still communicate with some of them after fifty-five years. I could share some very interesting and funny stories about my friends and

VIP'S, but maybe in another book. Most of my time served was spent in Europe. After receiving a separation from the Navy in 1955 I served four more years in the reserves and then received an Honorable discharge.

After my tour in the Navy I finished my High School education, and worked for a short period of time in the textile and auto industries. Then I joined the DuPont Company and spent 35 years in the manufacturing of several different chemicals. I enjoyed those years and met some nice people. With God's guidance I was promoted three times during that period of time and enjoyed traveling for the company on quite a few occasions.